Vanished Boyhood

THE AZRIELI SERIES OF HOLOCAUST SURVIVOR MEMOIRS: PREVIOUSLY PUBLISHED TITLES

Vanished Boyhood

George Stern

THE AZRIELI FOUNDATION
www.azrielifoundation.org

Cover and book design by Mark Goldstein
Endpaper maps by Martin Gilbert
Map on page xxvii by François Blanc

LIBRARY AND ARCHIVES CANADA CATALOGUING IN PUBLICATION

Stern, George, 1931–
        Vanished boyhood/ George Stern.

(Azrieli series of Holocaust survivor memoirs. Series V)
Includes bibliographical references and index.
ISBN 978-1-897470-34-3

1. Stern, George, 1931–. 2. Jews – Hungary – Biography. 3. Holocaust, Jewish (1939–1945) – Hungary – Personal narratives. 4. Holocaust survivors – Canada – Biography. I. Title. II. Series: Azrieli series of Holocaust survivor memoirs. Series V

DS135.H93S74 2013   940.53'18092   C2013-901364-4

FSC — MIX — From responsible sources — FSC® C004191

PRINTED IN CANADA

The Azrieli Series of Holocaust Survivor Memoirs

Contents

Series Preface:
In their own words...

In telling these stories, the writers have liberated themselves. For so many years we did not speak about it, even when we became free people living in a free society. Now, when at last we are writing about what happened to us in this dark period of history, knowing that our stories will be read and live on, it is possible for us to feel truly free. These unique historical documents put a face on what was lost, and allow readers to grasp the enormity of what happened to six million Jews – one story at a time.

David J. Azrieli, C.M., C.Q., M.Arch
Holocaust survivor and founder, The Azrieli Foundation

Since the end of World War II, over 30,000 Jewish Holocaust survivors have immigrated to Canada. Who they are, where they came from, what they experienced and how they built new lives for themselves and their families are important parts of our Canadian heritage. The Azrieli Foundation's Holocaust Survivor Memoirs Program was established to preserve and share the memoirs written by those who survived the twentieth-century Nazi genocide of the Jews of Europe and later made their way to Canada. The program is guided by the conviction that each survivor of the Holocaust has a remarkable story to tell, and that such stories play an important role in education about tolerance and diversity.

Millions of individual stories are lost to us forever. By preserving the stories written by survivors and making them widely available to a broad audience, the Azrieli Foundation's Holocaust Survivor Memoirs Program seeks to sustain the memory of all those who perished at the hands of hatred, abetted by indifference and apathy. The personal accounts of those who survived against all odds are as different as the people who wrote them, but all demonstrate the courage, strength, wit and luck that it took to prevail and survive in such terrible adversity. The memoirs are also moving tributes to people – strangers and friends – who risked their lives to help others, and who, through acts of kindness and decency in the darkest of moments, frequently helped the persecuted maintain faith in humanity and courage to endure. These accounts offer inspiration to all, as does the survivors' desire to share their experiences so that new generations can learn from them.

The Holocaust Survivor Memoirs Program collects, archives and publishes these distinctive records and the print editions are available free of charge to libraries, educational institutions and Holocaust-education programs across Canada, and at Azrieli Foundation educational events. They are also available for sale to the general public at bookstores.

The Azrieli Foundation would like to express appreciation to the following people for their invaluable efforts in producing this book: Sherry Dodson (Maracle Press), Sir Martin Gilbert, Farla Klaiman, David Sherman, Mia Spiro, Keaton Taylor, and Margie Wolfe and Emma Rodgers of Second Story Press.

About the Glossary

The following memoir contains a number of terms, concepts and historical references that may be unfamiliar to the reader. For information on major organizations; significant historical events and people; geographical locations; religious and cultural terms; and foreign-language words and expressions that will help give context and background to the events described in the text, please see the glossary beginning on page 105.

Introduction

Barely a month before George Stern's highly anticipated bar mitzvah in April 1944, the Nazis invaded Hungary and closed the synagogue where it was to be held. As Stern writes in his brave and poignant memoir, family and Jewish traditions were a central part of his happy childhood surrounded by his close-knit Orthodox Jewish family. Born György Stern in Újpest (New Pest), a largely Jewish suburb of Budapest where his father ran a wine business with his two brothers, he grew up next door to his paternal grandparents and opens his memoir with affectionate memories of extended family celebrations of Passover. Once that life is wiped away by the terrors of World War II, that lost bar mitzvah stayed with George Stern as the symbol of his vanished boyhood.

The Hungary that George Stern was born into in 1931 was still reeling from the outcome of World War I, the dissolution of the Austro-Hungarian Empire and the harsh territorial settlement imposed on Hungary at Versailles by the 1920 Treaty of Trianon. Viewed as nothing less than a catastrophe and known by Hungarians even today as the "Trianon trauma," the settlement triggered a shift away from the liberalism and tolerance that had characterized Hungary for a century before the war.

Throughout the nineteenth century, Hungary had followed a general trend toward reform and liberalism exemplified in part by the largely failed Revolutions of 1848 that swept through Western and Central Europe. Despite the collapse of the Hungarian Revolution of 1848, the reforms that followed were unparalleled elsewhere in east-central Europe. Most significant was the Austro-Hungarian Compromise of 1867, which peacefully negotiated Hungary's status as a sovereign kingdom no longer subject to the Austrian Empire and brought new rights of citizenship to the myriad national groups within the former empire.

Among the national, ethnic and religious groups to benefit from these nineteenth-century trends toward liberalism were Hungary's Jewish population, and Jewish assimilation was far more rapid in Hungary than in any other states of Central and Eastern Europe. While Újpest, where George and his family lived, was founded in 1835 by Jewish families who could not obtain licenses to operate their businesses in the capital, by 1895, when the Law of Reception was passed, Judaism was included on an equal basis among the recognized religions of Hungary. By the end of the nineteenth century, Jews no longer had to be identified in national statistics as a separate ethnic group, and the aim of Hungarian liberalism and of the liberal nobility who governed until 1918 was the "complete civic and political equality of Jews with the Christian population as proclaimed in paragraph 1 of the Emancipation Law."[1]

Jews have lived in the Carpathian Basin with few interruptions for one thousand years, but mass immigration only began in the late eighteenth century. From a population of 80,000 in 1787, the number of Jews tripled by 1840. During the Revolution of 1848, in which Hungarians rose up against their Habsburg rulers, the growing Jewish population in Hungary identified with the national cause

---

1 Paul Lendvai, *The Hungarians: A Thousand Years of Victory in Defeat* (Princeton: Princeton University Press, 2003), 330.

of the Magyars, the dominant ethnic group, the Hungarian language and, to a great extent, Hungarian culture. In the years following the Austro-Hungarian Compromise of 1867 that led to full civil and political rights for Jews, the Jewish population doubled to about half a million and then reached 911,000 in 1910. At this time, Jews made up 5 per cent of Hungary's population and about 7 per cent of Magyars belonged to the Jewish faith.[2] Significantly, 705,000 of them – more than 75 per cent – declared Hungarian to be their mother tongue.

Despite their relatively small proportion of the population, by 1910 almost half the lawyers and medical practitioners, more than 40 per cent of the journalists, more than 30 per cent of the engineers, and 25 per cent of artists and writers in Hungary were Jews. As the city of Budapest grew and became a commercial and cultural centre, it attracted Jewish merchants, traders and, later, skilled workers and intellectuals to the metropolis and they in turn contributed to the flourishing of the Hungarian capital. They were instrumental in economic progress and the implementation of industrialization. The cultural, scientific, financial and professional influence of the Jews was in no small measure responsible for Budapest becoming the greatest financial and media centre of Europe east of Vienna.

The end of World War I and the breakup of the Austro-Hungarian Empire marked a turning point for all Hungarians, with especially dire consequences for Hungarian Jews. Under the terms of the peace settlement, Hungary lost two-thirds of its historic lands and one-third of ethnic Hungarians were partitioned to new countries created following World War I, namely Czechoslovakia and Yugoslavia, while Romania became much enlarged. The territorially diminished country was nominally a kingdom, although it was without a king, and the government was headed by Regent Miklós Horthy, an admi-

---

2   Ibid, 331

ral of the former Austro-Hungarian navy. Despite the fact that the now-landlocked country no longer had a navy, Horthy impressed Hungarians with his proud demeanour and right-wing politics. He promised to bring stability to the substantially reduced country and work for territorial revision.

The post–World War I settlement created enormous hardship and dislocation for Hungary and its entire population. The new borders brought chaos and massive unemployment to the region. In addition, the short-lived 1919 Communist Party takeover of Hungary occurred just as the peace talks were going on in Paris. This communist regime, organized and led by Béla Kun and his henchmen, created widespread fear of Hungary in the West. Within the country, the fact that Kun and many of his deputies were Jewish stirred antisemitic sentiments as Hungarians identified Jews with the Bolshevik coup. Looking back, it seems that Hungarians were also convinced that Kun's takeover of the country had fuelled the negative treatment of Hungary at the Paris peace talks. The Romanians, Czechs, Slovaks, Serbs, and Croats had convinced the victorious powers that if they were granted more territory, they would wipe Hungary clean of communism.

As a result of these events and others that would soon unfold, the Hungary of George Stern's youth was far from the tolerant and liberal society that had existed before World War I. Hungarians became insular, self-absorbed and angry. The rallying cry of the interwar period was "Nem, nem, soha" (No! No! Never!) – never would the nation allow the injustices of the altered borders to remain. Large numbers of Hungary's Jews lived in regions that were partitioned to the neighbouring countries as well, where they continued to demonstrate their loyalty to the Hungarian language and culture, much to the dismay and anger of the host countries. In rump Hungary, antisemitism spread, leading to the first of a series of *numerus clausus* laws (quotas) enacted in 1920 to limit the number of Jews allowed to participate in education and business.

In 1920–1921, an economic and trade alliance between Czech-oslovakia, Yugoslavia and Romania further isolated Hungary, hard-ened popular and leadership sentiment in favour of territorial revi-sion, and led to closer relations with Germany – also bitter and reeling from its treatment under the Versailles settlement. This culminated less than twenty years later in the Vienna Awards, in which Nazi Germany backed Hungary's re-annexation of parts of Czechoslovakia in November 1938 and a section of Subcarpathian Ruthenia in March 1939, and the cession of the northern part of Transylvania from Romania back to Hungary in August 1940. Finally, in April 1940, the northern part of Yugoslavia (Voivodina) was re-annexed to Hungary.

Living as he did in the blissful community of extended family and neighbours in Jewish Újpest, young George was largely unaware of the currents roiling around him. Despite being allied with Nazi Germany, Hungary didn't officially enter World War II until, together with Nazi Germany and its allies, the country declared war on the Soviet Union in June 1941. Even then, George continued to lead the life of a typical eleven-year-old: attending school and Jewish scout camp and taking part in regular summer holidays at a kosher *pension* on Lake Balaton. He loved water sports and swam every day in the Olympic-sized pool on Margit Island in Budapest.

All around him, however, the geopolitical situation in Europe was growing increasingly fraught and soon many Hungarian men, includ-ing George's father and uncles, were conscripted into the Hungarian army; some were forced to do hard labour in the countryside and others, such as his uncle Manó, were sent to the Eastern Front. By engaging in a formal alliance with Nazi Germany, Horthy and his governing party had, as historian István Deák summarizes, taken on a difficult and divisive set of tasks: "To fight Bolshevism in every one of its manifestations, to rely on Germany for political, military and economic help; to reduce the Jewish presence in the economy and society, yet also to keep the domestic fascists at bay and to preserve

Hungarian independence vis-à-vis Nazi Germany."[3] It soon became apparent that Horthy's government had clearly miscalculated the high price the Nazi leadership would exact in repayment for the territories regained by Hungary.

One of Hungary's most adept anti-Nazi politicians, Miklós Kállay, who was appointed prime minister in 1942, maintained a clever balancing act between the ominous will of the Third Reich and the skeptical Allies that was known in contemporary political parlance as the *Kállay Kettős*, or Kállay Two-Step. Two steps to the right, then two steps back to the left brought the dancer to the original starting point: from 1938 to 1942, anti-Jewish laws were enacted in Hungary, but were watered down through weak enforcement.

Hungary's reluctance to deport its Jews became a decisive factor in the breakdown of German-Hungarian relations as the war continued. The Hungarian government dragged its feet on Hitler's demands to move Jews into ghettos, and Jews in Hungary were not required to wear the Star of David until after Germany occupied Hungary in March 1944. Summoned to meet with Hitler at Schloss Klessheim near Salzburg in April 1943 to discuss this very issue, Horthy was asked to explain his policies with regard to Hungary's Jews. Germany's foreign minister, Joachim von Ribbentrop, bluntly stated that the Jews should be exterminated or at least put in concentration camps. Hitler was quoted as admonishing Horthy that the Jewish question was "being solved least satisfactorily by the Hungarians." The obstacle, as the Nazis saw it, was that Horthy's family was "extraordinarily badly tangled up with the Jews" and Horthy would therefore continue to resist every effort to tackle the Jewish problem aggressively.[4]

By the spring of 1944, when the seventy-six-year-old Horthy was

---

3 István Deák, "A Fatal Compromise? The Debate over Collaboration and Resistance in Hungary," *The Politics of Retribution in Europe: World War II and Its Aftermath* (Princeton, NJ: Princeton University Press, 2000), 51.

4 Lendvai, 420.

called to a second meeting with Hitler at Schloss Klessheim and issued an ultimatum, a German defeat in the war seemed a likely outcome. Nonetheless, with Allied bombers already flying regular sorties
over Budapest and the Soviet army encroaching from the east, the
German Wehrmacht implemented "Plan Margarethe" and invaded
Hungary from the west on March 19, 1944. George Stern remembers
that day with great precision and poignantly details his first glimpse
of German Panzer tanks rolling through his city in his memoirs.
From that point on, Adolf Eichmann personally took control of the
"Final Solution" in Hungary. Within days, about three thousand pro-
Allied politicians, officials, aristocrats and intellectuals were arrested
and deported to Germany by the Gestapo and the collaborating
Hungarian police and gendarmerie.

In an appendix to his seminal work on the destruction of Hungarian
Jewry, *The Politics of Genocide: The Holocaust in Hungary*, Randolph
Braham enumerated 107 regulations decreed after the German invasion.[5] Along with the hundreds of thousands of Hungarian Jews,
George Stern and his family were now ordered to wear the Star of
David and all 11,000 Újpest Jews were forced to move into the small,
dirty and overcrowded Újpest ghetto. The ghetto was sealed but, taking a chance, George decided not to wear the yellow star and was
thus able to slip in and out. His father managed to buy him false papers that identified him as a Christian youth, and sent George and his
cousin Vera to the countryside to work on a farm near Soltvadkert
in south-central Hungary. In order not to attract the attention of the
authorities, the whole family couldn't go there together.

Nowhere else in Central and Eastern Europe had more than
800,000 Jews (including converts to Christianity) been able to live so

---

5 Randolph L. Braham, *The Politics of Genocide: The Holocaust in Hungary,* Vol. 2
(New York: Columbia University Press, 1981).

long in relative safety as they had in Hungary.[6] But, as historian Paul Lendvai also writes, "Nowhere else in Central and Eastern Europe were the Jews sent to their death so quickly and so brutally."[7] Under the supervision of Adolf Eichmann and his thugs, starting on May 15, 1944, Hungarian gendarmes first implemented the deportation to Auschwitz-Birkenau of Jews from Sub-Carpathian Ruthenia and northern Transylvania. When this was completed, they began the systematic deportation of the Jews from northern, southeastern and western Hungary, as well as from the southern regions. The transport of Hungarian Jews from all the regions outside of Budapest was organized in less than two months. They were herded into windowless cattle cars, seventy people to a car, each car given one pail of drinking water and one pail for excrement. The Hungarians in charge of the transports reported to their German masters that between May 15 and July 7, they had expedited 147 trains to Auschwitz, containing 437,402 Jews. [8]

According to the schedule developed by interior ministry planners, the Jews of Budapest were to be the last group sent to be killed. As police began relocating Jews in the capital city into specially designated "yellow star" houses, a group of advisors around Horthy began to consider halting the deportations, a decision the regent finally took on July 7. Only the Jews of Budapest and about 150,000 Jewish men between the ages of eighteen and forty-eight who had been conscripted into labour battalions, among them George Stern's father, remained in Hungary after July 1944. Paradoxically, although the men in the labour battalions faced terrible conditions, a large proportion of them survived the war.[9]

In terms of assessing what Horthy knew at the time and what his

---

6 This number fluctuated due to territorial changes.

7 Lendvai, 422.

8 Lendvai, 422.

9 Deák, 65.

role as regent was, István Deák has described the feelings of pow-erlessness to stop the deportations that Horthy wrote about in his memoir. Even so, Horthy writes, the deportations were carried out by Eichmann, not by Hungarians, and he had no idea where they were being sent. About the latter point, Deák takes issue with Horthy's version of history: "As far as his lack of power was concerned, that was probably true, but everything else was a lie. He had found out in good time what Auschwitz signified, but preferred to ignore it." Still, Deák argues that, by the summer of 1944, Horthy did try to help the remaining Jews of Budapest:

When it was their turn in June/July 1944 he ordered military action against the gendarmes, who, as he feared, were also planning a coup against him. In the event more than 40% of Hungarian Jews survived. Horthy was not a monster, but he was not humanitarian either. He was no democrat but never tried to be a dictator. He claimed to have been a lifelong anti-Semite. Still, under his reign and despite the deportations, more Jews survived the Nazi terror than any other country in Hitler's Europe.[10]

On October 15, 1944, with the Red Army already inside the Carpathian Mountains on Hungary's northeast border, Horthy tried to extricate Hungary from the war. After concluding an armistice with Moscow, the regent declared Hungary's "defection" from the war. The so-called defection, however, was poorly planned and ex-ecuted – Horthy seemed to genuinely believe that he could cause such a turnaround by merely issuing a proclamation over the radio without appropriate military and political preparation. Moreover, his government, and the upper ranks of the military in particular, were

10 István Deák, "Nikolaus von Horthy, Admiral und Reichsverweser" in *Europaische Rundschau*, Vienna 94/2, 71–85.

rife with people spying for Nazi Germany. The Nazis uncovered the plans and an SS commando led by Otto Skorzeny kidnapped Horthy's son on the day of the attempted capitulation. In order to achieve his son's release, Horthy was forced to withdraw his proclamation and legalize the takeover of the government by the extreme right-wing leader of the Arrow Cross Party, Ferenc Szálasi.

As these events unfolded, George and his cousin Vera were still living on the farm. When they heard about Horthy's radio address along with the welcome news that this might mean the end of the war, they took the long, arduous train journey back home to the capital. It was only when they arrived that they heard the shocking news of the takeover by Szálasi and his supporters. George and Vera had mistakenly returned to the most dangerous place for Jews in Hungary.

The Arrow Cross reign of terror claimed the lives of untold numbers of Jews during the final months of the war. Almost as soon as Szálasi was instated, Arrow Cross goons grabbed Jews in the streets and went on a killing spree. Many were shot on the Danube embankment, their bodies tossed into the river; when the killers ran low on bullets, they tied Jews together and threw them into the icy water in twos and threes. This way, they only had to use one shot per group; as the dead plunged into the river they would pull the others down with them. Still other people were hanged along city avenues and in parks. Added to these were the victims of the notorious death marches to Austria organized by Adolf Eichmann. Desperate for workers, the Germans ordered Szálasi to send 50,000 able-bodied Jews to Austria as forced labour brigades. Between November 6 and December 1, 1944, the fascist Arrow Cross regime forced tens of thousands of Jews to travel hundreds of kilometres on foot from Budapest to Hegyeshalom on the Austrian border in freezing conditions.

In Budapest, large crowds of Jews tried desperately to gain entrance to safe houses organized by foreign diplomats such as Raoul Wallenberg of the Swedish embassy, or the staff at the Swiss embassy, the Papal Nuncio and other embassies, who worked feverishly to hand out as many protection papers as possible. Despite their efforts, the diplomatic protection was often ignored by the Arrow Cross.[11]

Even as the Nazis were in retreat, they and the Arrow Cross issued directives that Budapest be defended house by house, and the capital city paid a high price as a result. The bridges over the Danube connecting the two parts of the city were blown up by the retreating German army. Many parts of the city were levelled and many thousands of homes destroyed. As a result of this "scorched earth" policy, tens of thousands more civilians as well as Hungarian, German and Soviet soldiers died as Budapest became a front line of battle. At the moment when Nazi Germany's defeat was almost a fait accompli, it is estimated that more than 50,000 Jews were victims of the Arrow Cross regime's reign of terror. At least 25,000 Jews did manage to survive in the capital, either with false papers or through being hidden by friends and non-Jewish relatives. George Stern was one of those who survived through cunning, bravery and sheer luck. Many members of his family, including his mother, were not as fortunate.

In Budapest, the fighting continued until February 13, 1945, when, after a six-week siege, the last German soldier was killed or captured. The end of hostilities in all of Hungary finally took place on April 4. Because of the many border changes that occurred during and after the war, historians can only offer rough estimates of the true human cost of the war to Hungarian Jews. The number of Jewish victims was likely 564,000 in the Greater Hungary of 1941, with more than 100,000 in Budapest alone.[12] The difficulties of compiling these figures with any precision is further exacerbated by the fact that an unknown number of Jews who were driven out or survived the

---

11 For further information on the safe houses and the precarious lives of Jews in Budapest during this period see Anna Porter, *Kasztner's Train: The True Story of Rezso Kasztner, Unknown Hero of the Holocaust* (Vancouver, BC: Douglas & McIntyre, 2007).

12 Lendvai, 425

death camps never returned to Hungary, but emigrated directly to Palestine, Canada, the United States or other countries.

According to Deák, the fact that, "The Hungarian government protected the Jews until the 19th of March 1944 and then again between August and October meant that the Germans and Hungarian Nazis had very little time to proceed with the Final Solution, the shortest time available for this undertaking anywhere in Axis Europe." This, he argues, largely accounts for the 40 per cent survival rate of Hungarian Jews. [13]

Still, by the end of World War II, it has been estimated that some 900,000 people, or slightly more than 6 per cent of Hungary's population, died or were killed during the war.[14] More than 600,000 were captured by the Soviets and 300,000 soldiers surrendered to British and US troops. Many of these men and young boys later died in harsh Soviet gulags and from disease and poor conditions in US-run prisoner-of-war camps.

The arrival of the Red Army further compounded Hungary's woes. While the Soviets liberated political prisoners and Jews, they also committed acts of looting and mass rape. Estimates of how many Hungarian women, including Hungarian Jewish women, were brutalized by the Soviet army vary. Untold numbers (estimates range from 50,000 to 200,000) were assaulted in front of their families, husbands and children. There was no one to whom such crimes could be reported as the Soviets were in control of the post-war Hungarian government.

The Soviet army further terrorized the population by arresting and dragging away countless civilians, both men and women, usually for no apparent reason. Referred to as "Malenkij Robota," meaning "little work," most were shipped off to labour camps in the

---

13 István Deák, "A Fatal Compromise?, 66.

14 Lendvai, 425.

Soviet Union. Again, precise statistics are almost impossible to de-
termine. Red Army soldiers showed little interest in distinguishing
one Hungarian citizen from another and documentation really didn't
help as most Soviet soldiers could only read the Cyrillic alphabet.
Jews who participated in underground communist organizations and
Jewish survivors of the Nazi camps were as likely as the rest to fall
victim, as were captured Hungarian soldiers and Jewish forced labourers. Most never returned.

Within a few years of the end of the war, the Soviets amalgamated
their power and installed a Communist regime in Hungary. As with
the other nations of Eastern and Central Europe, Hungary was controlled as a satellite of the Soviet Union and, in keeping with Soviet
policies, the memory of the Holocaust was glossed over for the more
than fifty years of Communist rule, talked of only in general terms
and lumped in with other "crimes of fascism."

George Stern had survived, but as a young teenager in 1945,
he concluded that there was only more turmoil ahead. In 1948, he
grabbed the opportunity to leave the country with a group of young
Jews destined for Palestine. After many adventures and twists and
turns of fate that he describes with a storyteller's sense of narrative,
he finally made his home in Canada in 1970.

In the post-Communist era, beginning in 1989, Hungary has
started the painful task of facing the dark and hidden chapters of its
history. In 2004, a state-funded National Museum and Archives dedicated to the memory of the Holocaust opened in Budapest, the fifth
national Holocaust Museum in the world at the time. At the opening,
Prime Minister Péter Medgyessy admitted for the first time that the
"Hungarian Holocaust was a heinous crime committed by Hungarian
people against Hungarian people."[15]

---

15 The museum was opened on April 27, 2004.

George Stern's admirable memoir is an important addition to the growing body of knowledge and memory of the Holocaust in Hungary. His account of what happened to him and his family connects the Old World and the New, and illuminates his experiences so that future generations can better understand this traumatic era.

Susan M. Papp
University of Toronto
2013

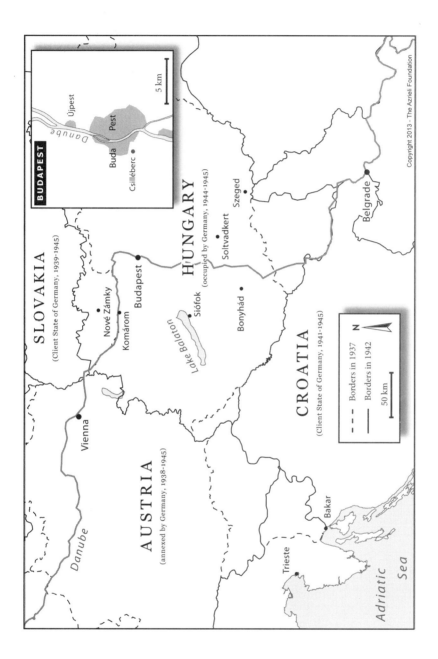

SLOVAKIA
(Client State of Germany, 1939-1945)

HUNGARY
(occupied by Germany, 1944-1945)

CROATIA
(Client State of Germany, 1941-1945)

AUSTRIA
(annexed by Germany, 1938-1945)

Vienna

Nové Zámky

Komárom

Budapest

Lake Balaton

Siófok

Bonyhád

Soltvadkert

Szeged

Belgrade

Danube

Bakar

Trieste

Adriatic

Sea

N

Borders in 1937

Borders in 1942

50 km

BUDAPEST

Danube

Újpest

Buda

Pest

Csilléberc

5 km

George Stern's Family Tree*
(Note: The paternal and maternal Sterns were not related)

PATERNAL GRANDPARENTS:
Fülöp Stern m. *Bertha Fleischman*

UNCLE:
Jenő m. *Lili* ——— *Iván*

UNCLE:
Sándor m. *Erzsi* ——— *Tibor*
remarried *Olga*

UNCLE:
Manó m. *Kato*

AUNT:
Aranka m. *Frici* ┬── *Vera*
                    └── *Tomàs*

UNCLE:
Àrmin m. *Sosanna* ┬── *Nurit*
                     └── *Nizza*

FATHER:
Ernő m.

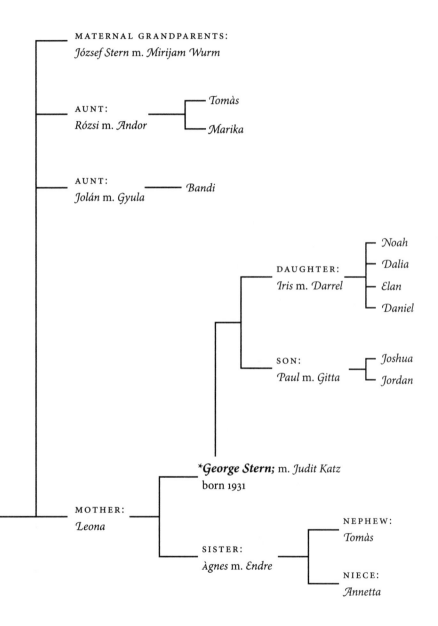

MATERNAL GRANDPARENTS:
József Stern m. Mirijam Wurm

AUNT:
Rózsi m. Andor
— Tomàs
— Marika

AUNT:
Jolán m. Gyula
— Bandi

DAUGHTER:
Iris m. Darrel
— Noah
— Dalia
— Elan
— Daniel

SON:
Paul m. Gitta
— Joshua
— Jordan

*George Stern; m. Judit Katz
born 1931

MOTHER:
Leona

SISTER:
Àgnes m. Endre

NEPHEW:
Tomàs

NIECE:
Annetta

Foreword

Six million murdered and millions more intended victims who miraculously escaped. While the fate of the victims was the same – death – the events that led to that death were quite different.

With each survivor of the Shoah comes a unique story. Some are stories of courage in the face of unimaginable evil; some are stories of resilience and resistance; some are stories of profound suffering and unspeakable death; and others are stories of ingenuity. Each story is different and reflects the special circumstances that the survivor encountered, told in a way that captures his or her unique experiences.

George Stern tells his story in a remarkably unexpected way. It is almost nonchalant and yet powerfully dramatic and poignant. It is a story about the loss of innocence and a stolen youth. It is a story about overcoming hate and persecution. It is a story about the fall of Budapest to the Nazis and their sympathizers and the struggle of one family to save their dignity and humanity as well as their lives.

It is a story that we read with trepidation. For even though we know that George Stern lives to tell the tale, it is a cogent reminder that millions of other Jews could not do the same.

Rabbi Wayne Allen
Beth Tikvah, Toronto

To my wife, Judit, who has always stood beside me, and for helping me choose the pictures. I love you.

To my children, Paul-Pinchas Stern and Iris Yashinsky. I could not ask God for better children.

To Jordan Stern and Noah Yashinsky – my two eldest grandsons. Both of you inspired and motivated me to write this and without you I would not have been able to do it.

To my other lovely grandchildren: Joshua Stern, Dalia Leona Yashinsky, Elan Yashinsky and Daniel Yashinsky. I wrote this so that you would know about our family roots and the Holocaust – the most horrific time of any Jew's life – and to show you that in the darkest days of my life, God was always with me. You all give me a lot of happiness and joy and I love all of you.

I am also grateful to Jean Yashinsky, whose advice and suggestions helped me and encouraged me to write. I would not have been able to write without your support and dedication.

I hope that this book will show my grandchildren the right road to walk and that they will learn from it.

I love you all.

Your husband, your father, your szaba,
George Stern
Spring 2002

If the statistics are right, the Jews constitute but one per cent of the human race. It suggests a nebulous dim puff of star-dust lost in the blaze of the Milky Way. Properly the Jew ought hardly to be heard of; but he is heard of, has always been heard of. He is as prominent on the planet as any other people, and, his commercial importance is extravagantly out of proportion to the smallness of his bulk. His contributions to the world's list of great names in literature, science, art, music, finance, medicine, and abstruse learning are also away out of proportion to the weakness of his numbers.

He has made marvellous fight in this world, in all the ages; and has done it with his hands tied behind him. He could be vain of himself, and be excused for it. The Egyptian, the Babylonian, and the Persian rose, filled the planet with sound and splendor, then faded to dream-stuff and passed away; the Greek and the Roman followed, and made a vast noise, and they are gone; other peoples have sprung up and held their torch high for a time, but it burned out, and they sit in twilight now, or have vanished.

The Jew saw them all, beat them all, and is now what he always was, exhibiting no decadence, no infirmities of age, no weakening of his parts, no slowing of his energies, no dulling of his alert and aggressive mind. All things are mortal but the Jew; all other forces pass, but he remains. What is the secret of his immortality?

Mark Twain,
excerpt from "Concerning the Jews,"
Harper's Magazine, March 1898

The Early Years

As I started to write this memoir, spring was approaching and, with it, the holiday of Pesach, or Passover[1]. I don't remember everything from my childhood, but some things, like the Passover holiday, were so special that the memories are very clear to me.

One Passover tradition asks that if people can afford to, they provide those less fortunate with foods that are eaten during the holiday, like matzah, eggs, chicken or wine. My father, Ernő, and Uncle Jenő kept that tradition by putting aside one barrel of kosher wine from their vineyard. Just before Passover, poor families could come to our courtyard, where our wine store was located, and collect as much wine as they needed. When I was eight years old, I was given the honour of giving out the wine to them and I filled the bottles they brought, one by one. This took almost the whole day because we gave away a few hundred litres of wine, but I was glad to do it because it was a mitzvah, a good deed.

---

1 For information on Passover, as well as on other religious and cultural terms; major organizations; significant historical events and people; geographical locations; and foreign-language words and expressions contained in the text, please see the glossary.

Our seder was always conducted in the house of my paternal grandfather, Fülöp Stern, where, most of the time, our large extended family gathered. My grandparents, Fülöp and Bertha, had six children – my father, Ernő, Aunt Aranka, and my uncles Jenő, Sándor, Manó and Àrmin. I have vivid memories of those seders with my parents, Ernő and Leona, and my older sister, Ágnes, along with Aunt Aranka, Uncle Frici and cousins Vera and Tomàs; Uncle Jenő, Aunt Lili and cousin Iván; and Uncles Sándor and Manó and Àrmin, who was the youngest. According to tradition, everyone drinks four cups of wine on seder nights. My sister, Ágnes, who was five years older than me, somehow always managed to drink more; she would get drunk and laugh and jump around and make noise, interfering with my grandfather's singing of the Haggadah, which I found pretty funny. She was sent to the kitchen or outside to the garden to clear her head so many times.

My memory of my uncle Friedlander Frigyes, whom we called Frici, is quite different. He came from Mátészalka, a region in eastern Hungary, and his family, many of whom were rabbis, were very religious. Uncle Frici had a special custom during the seder prayer asking God to take us out of slavery, out of Egypt, to freedom. The people of Israel sang this prayer after they crossed the Red Sea by foot and saw the Egyptian army destroyed by the waves. When we were about to start the prayer, Uncle Frici would go outside and return with a wooden bathtub. He put it in the middle of the room where we were all sitting and filled the bathtub with plenty of water. Then, as we prayed, mentioning the miracle of crossing the sea, he got in the tub and crossed it a few times, symbolizing how Moses, with the help of God, parted the sea.

I was around six years old the first time we saw my uncle do this and we were all stunned because we had never done that at our seder. My father and Uncle Jenő couldn't help laughing at him, which really hurt his feelings. It took a few months for him to get over it.

~

I was born on April 21, 1931, at the Horthy-Miklós Street Hospital in Újpest, Hungary. According to my birth certificate, my name was registered as György (George), and the doctor who delivered me was Csizmadia Zsigmond. The document also stated that my father was Ernő Stern, thirty-four years old and Jewish. My mother, Leona Bina (Pnina) Stern, twenty-nine years old and also Jewish. So, of course, I was born Jewish. At the time, birth certificates, as well as other official personal documents like school registration cards and passports, were inscribed with the person's religion.

Újpest, which translates to New Pest, was a suburb of Budapest that was founded by two Jewish families in 1835 on land rented to them by Count István Károlyi. The head of one of the founding families was Izsák Lőwy who, along with his two brothers, was a leather-goods manufacturer of coats, hats, vests and gloves.

The Lőwys had wanted to settle in Budapest, but the city laws at the time didn't allow Jews to get licences to operate their businesses in the capital. Instead, they decided to establish a new community close by. Újpest was ten kilometres from Budapest and received official status as a village. For the first thirty-five years of its existence, all the municipality's official records, including land and birth registrations, were written partly in Hebrew and partly in Yiddish.

In 1854, the first rabbi and children's teacher in Újpest was Markus Stern, who was not related to our family. The first Orthodox synagogue was built in 1839 on Bocskai Street and the larger Neolog synagogue on József Street was built in 1866 and still exists today. The Neolog synagogue's members numbered approximately nine thousand, and about one thousand Jews, including my family, belonged to the smaller Orthodox synagogue. When I was growing up, Újpest's population was about 70,000, including about 11,000 Jews.

From 1927 to 1944, the chief rabbi of Újpest was Dr. Dénes Friedmann, the great-grandson of the famous Rebbe Chasam Sofer from Bratislava. Rabbi Friedmann completed rabbinical school at the Rabbinical Seminary of Budapest, which was, and remains, in my opinion, the best rabbinical school in Europe.

Rabbi Friedmann was an excellent spiritual leader and a great humanitarian – an extraordinarily good person who was the soul and hope of the congregation. His one son, Emil, was about my age and my family knew Rabbi Friedmann well. The rabbi was a modern conservative with a tremendous knowledge of the Talmud and the Bible. My mother loved to go to synagogue on Friday night or Sabbath morning to hear his sermons. I often went with her and I still remember his beautifully expressed words of hope and his lectures on Jewish traditions. When he spoke, the whole congregation was silent, listening to every word. He was young – he was ordained at twenty-four – but the congregation respected him. Rabbi Friedmann always said that if bad times came, he would never abandon his congregation. Many rabbis said that but didn't always keep their word. Rabbi Friedmann meant what he said – he never left his people. In 1944, when the Nazis started deporting the Jews from Újpest, they killed the rabbi's son right in front of him and then deported Rabbi Friedmann and his wife to Auschwitz, where he died, along with so many of his fellow Jews, at the age of forty-two.

~

My family lived in a house on 26 József Street beside my grandparents' house, on the same street as the Neolog synagogue. Most of the bungalows on the street were the same style and we leased a modest two-bedroom bungalow, with low windows at street level, from a family named Sindlovitch. They had two daughters and I had a crush on one of them. Our house had a big courtyard, beside which were the office and warehouse for my father's wine business.

The front half of the house my grandparents lived in was a bakery that sold Jewish breads like challah and dark rye. Every Friday, we took our typical Saturday lunch of *cholent* – white beans, barley, hard-boiled eggs and pieces of beef or goose – to the bakery oven to cook slowly overnight. That was our tradition because, being Orthodox, we could not cook on Shabbat. Saturday at noon, I would go with a small wagon to pick it up. It was always delicious, with the top slightly burned and the eggs turned completely brown.

My grandfather, Fülöp Pinchas Stern, was a pleasant, gentle person and, according to my father and Aunt Lili, he loved me the best of all his grandchildren because I was the only grandchild willing to go to synagogue with him. He was observant and walked twice a day to the shul for morning prayers (Shacharit), and afternoon and evening prayers (Mincha and Maariv). Every evening as I walked with him to the synagogue, he held my hand and talked to me slowly. I can understand now why my grandfather was happy that I went with him to shul because I enjoy the same happiness when my grandchildren do the same with me.

My paternal grandmother, Bertha, came from the small village of Csév, not far from Budapest. Grandma Bertha had a strong character and loved to work, traits that my father inherited. She seemed to be constantly on the move except, of course, when she was sleeping; I rarely saw her sit down for a long conversation with anybody. Not only was she a hard worker, but she saved money and was a careful spender, except when it came to the education of her children. She was a good cook too, although the best cook in our family was my mother. Even Grandma Bertha asked my mother for recipes, especially for her homemade matzah balls, and baking and cooking advice. But Bertha did make the best fruit preserves and cucumbers in town. Her summer preserves were made with cherries, plums, apricots, and sour cherries with rum, and she kept them throughout the whole winter in her cold storage room in one-, two-, three- and five-litre jars.

She only opened those jars on Shabbat or special family occasions but her grandchildren – especially me and my cousins Tomàs and Vera – loved her sour cucumbers too much to wait for a family gathering. So one day, when I was around eight years old, we decided that we had to do something to get those tasty cucumbers earlier and we all agreed to slowly steal them. But how would we do that and have our grandma Bertha not discover the theft?

We soon came up with a solution: in her storage room there was a long, high shelf where she put the jars in three lines, like soldiers, until the shelves were all filled up. There were dozens and dozens of jars full of different preserves. So, when our grandmother left the house to go somewhere for the day we, under my command, went to the storage room, took one jar of cucumbers from the middle line, opened it and ate them all. Then we washed the empty jar to get rid of the vinegar smell and replaced the empty jar in the third line, which our grandmother could not see without using a ladder, since she was rather short. We did this during summer and fall and by the winter, the second and third line of jars were almost empty.

When, at Chanukah, the first winter holiday, she discovered what we had done, she shouted at us and started to chase us, but we ran away. She was so agitated that she fainted. The doctor said that she had a nervous heart condition – the old term for an irregular heartbeat.

Another memorable event with her fruit jars occurred one New Year's Eve, when the whole family gathered in my grandmother's home to eat and drink and have a good time. At the height of the celebration, Grandma Bertha went to her famous storage room and came back with a jar of cherries and rum, which we all loved. It looked fine from the outside, but when she opened it, she discovered that there was mould in the jar. Her food rarely spoiled. She took the jar outside to the courtyard where she raised chickens and geese, and she threw all those fermented rum cherries into the garden. She came back and opened another jar of the same dessert and it was delicious. We ate the whole thing and some of us got a little drunk from it. After midnight, when the night ended and we were leaving, we saw that all the geese and the chickens in the courtyard looked drunk, as if they were dancing with each other! I guess they had a good time celebrating New Year's, too. We called Grandma outside to see what was happening and it was the first time we saw her laugh. That was a night I will never forget.

My maternal grandmother, Mirijam, died before I was born, but we visited my grandfather József in Bonyhád, a town in southwestern Hungary about two hundred kilometres from Újpest, every summer for two or three weeks. My grandfather, whom I remember as quite a sweet old man, lived in a bungalow with a long backyard and in the front of the house he had a vinegar and wine retail store open to the public. He was pretty quiet and he liked to sit in a chair in front of the house for hours at a time. His daughter, Rózsi, her husband, Andor, and their two children, Tomàs and Marika, lived with him. My cousin Tomàs was about my age and we had a fun time together.

Every summer before we left Bonyhád we stopped at the nearby farm of my Aunt Jolán, my mother's other sister. Aunt Jolán and Uncle Gyula had one son, my cousin Bandi, who was a strong farm boy one year older than me. They had a lot of chickens and geese on their farm and whenever we came to visit, my aunt cooked a dinner of fried chicken with about ten young chickens. Whenever my cousin and I started to eat them, we would have a fun contest to see who could eat the most. I won most of the time and once I even ate two to three whole chickens! We usually stayed at the farm for one or two days and then headed back to Budapest by bus.

In 1936, when I was five and a half years old, my father wanted to send me to cheder, a Jewish religious school. All the Orthodox Jewish boys went to cheder to learn the five books of Moses. But there was one problem – I told my father that I didn't want to go. He took me anyway, but I ran away and came home much earlier than the other boys. I didn't like it there because the teachers shouted at us and sometimes beat us. The next day, my father took me back and I did the same thing. The third day, my father put me into a potato sack and took me once more to cheder, but I ran away again. Finally, he gave up and I didn't have to go anymore.

My elementary school, which was for Jewish students only, was on the corner near my home, just two houses from my grandparents' house, in a one-storey building with a courtyard large enough for about a hundred and fifty children. My favourite sports were soccer and running. I ran so fast that I was the best one-hundred- and two-hundred-metre sprinter in the school. I often raced the streetcars along Árpád Street, the main street, and would get ahead of them, which was great fun. When I was ten years old, I came to love swimming as well and I always swam in the mornings before I got to my junior high school in Budapest. Újpest didn't have a Jewish junior high school. I woke up every day at 5:30 a.m., swam from 6:30 a.m. to 7:15 a.m., and then went to class at 8:00 a.m. I swam in the Olympic-sized pool at Margit Island, an island in central Budapest in the middle of the Danube River. The swimming pool was used to train Olympic swimmers and the water-polo team, which was the best in the world.

During part of the summer vacation my family went to Lake Balaton, the biggest and most famous lake in Hungary – it was approximately fourteen kilometres wide and seventy kilometres long. We rented a room in a kosher pension in Siófok, a city on the south shore of the lake and the birthplace of the famous Jewish composer Emmerich Kálmán. I swam a lot there, but my favourite water sport was kayaking. The water was usually beautifully clear, but the lake could become stormy suddenly and produce huge, dangerous waves. Over the years, many boats were lost in the Balaton. When a storm approached, cannon shots were fired to let the boats know to get to shore as fast as possible.

For another part of the summer I went to camp with the Jewish scout group to a lake called Velencei-tó, a shallow and muddy lake full of blood-sucking leeches. I earned my first real money at this camp. After being there for three weeks with the other hundred or so boys, I realized that hardly any of them had brought envelopes, stamps or postcards to write home to their parents. So the next year, before I left for camp, I bought lots of envelopes, papers, stamps and postcards with the small amount I had earned at odd jobs and from the small allowance my father gave me, and took them with me to sell at double the price. This worked out really well – the campers could write home and I had earned some money. Other than that, I didn't like the camp much because there weren't any girls. I preferred our Siófok vacations, where there were lots of girls my age and older who came from wealthy families in Budapest.

On Saturdays I went to shul, but Sundays I often went to the nearby Hármashatárhegy, the Three Border Mountain, which took about one hour by streetcar. I would climb and wander through the thick forest floor, where lots of small animals and birds lived, although I rarely saw them. The animals and birds hid from all the cruel people who shouted and chased them. I sometimes went to Hármashatárhegy with the boy scouts, but one Sunday morning, I woke up early as usual and decided to go with my cousin Iván. I ate breakfast, packed my backpack with some food and walked the ten minutes to Iván's house. When I arrived there and asked Aunt Lili where Iván was, she replied that he had already left to go to the forest. I asked her who he had gone there with and she replied that he had gone on his own. He was only about twelve years old but was allowed to go anywhere by himself.

In the summer of 1942, when I was eleven, I asked my father to find me a summer job. This pleased him and he soon found me a job with a man from our shul who was a chemical engineer. He was a short man whose home and small factory, where he manufactured his own patented shaving powder, was across the street from the shul. This powder, when mixed with water, became a thick shaving cream that men used to easily remove their beards with only a wooden knife. All the religious Jewish men had to use that method to abide by the Torah, where it is written that no sharp metal item, such as a razor, should touch the skin. That cream really worked – after two minutes with a wooden knife, which was not sharp at all, whiskers were gone.

His business was the only one in the city and it was pretty success-
ful – even though the cream smelled bad. At that time, of course,
there were no electric shavers. I worked in his factory for a few weeks,
filling up one-kilogram bags for retail but I didn't like it because the
white powder, like baker's flour, flew everywhere and I was always
covered with it. Also, the factory didn't get enough fresh air. I much
preferred working with the horses in my father's wine business, but I
wanted paid work and my father would not have paid me.

That same summer, while I was playing soccer with a bunch of
neighbourhood children, as I had done since I was six years old, the
Christian boys, who had lost the game, started to call me a "dirty Jew"
and four or five of them threatened to beat me up. We had all grown
up together, two or three Jewish boys and the rest Christians. As soon
as they got close to me, I gave two of them a strong kick in the area
where boys are most sensitive and quickly ran away. They couldn't
catch me because I was such a fast runner. This was just one example
of antisemitism in Hungary. It was taught in the Catholic schools, in
Christian homes and by priests in the churches. In my experience,
hatred of Jewish people was rampant in Hungary, and both children
and adults were completely poisoned with antisemitic beliefs.

Life Changes Overnight

March 19, 1944, was a regular, chilly spring morning. As always, I woke up early to travel the ten kilometres to my Jewish high school in Budapest, and walked along to Váci Street in Újpest to where it met Árpád Street, which went straight across the city from the shores of the Danube. But it soon turned out that this morning was not so regular at all.

When I was close to the streetcar station, which was about a ten-minute walk from my home, I saw a huge column of tanks travelling along Váci Street. I wasn't able to identify what type of tanks they were so I approached one of the men working in the station and asked him about them. He answered, "You don't know? The German army invaded Budapest during the night without any resistance from the Hungarian army!" I had never seen a German tank before, but it turned out that I had been looking at the famous German Panzer tanks.

Suddenly, during the next few weeks, the Nazis established many ominous edicts, including the order that every Jewish person had to put a yellow Magen David on every coat, dress or garment that was worn outside. I wasn't ashamed of my Jewishness, but I never wore the yellow star. I was a rebel and I couldn't bear the discrimination. Soon, Jews were not allowed to travel to any place outside Újpest city limits and the synagogues were closed. My bar mitzvah, which had been booked for Shabbat, April 22, at our small but intimate *shtiebl* on Árpád Street, never happened. I had gone there every evening with my grandfather to pray until the Nazis closed it. On my birthday, we celebrated what should have been just before my bar mitzvah day in our living room and we barely had a minyan. I didn't get any gifts, but I believed that God was watching out for us and that one day things would be better.

However, the hardships got worse every day. American planes frequently bombed Újpest, Budapest and Csepel, where there were armament and heavy vehicle factories that the Allies wanted to destroy. Groups of eighteen to twenty B-17s – four-engine planes also called Flying Fortresses – flying in a V-formation, carpet bombed large areas. The planes flew at altitudes that the Hungarian anti-aircraft guns couldn't reach. When they got close to Budapest, a loud siren sounded and everybody ran to the closest bunker or basement. Our house had a deep underground basement and everyone except me would sit there, sometimes for hours. I did go into the basement, but I only stayed ten or twenty minutes. As soon as I heard the airplane engines I ran upstairs to the garden to watch the bombers approaching. The planes looked like silver birds. It was dangerous and against regulations to go upstairs, but I wasn't scared. I prayed to God that those American planes would destroy the Nazis and the factories so we all could be free again. There were a lot of casualties; one bombing run was so close that the house shook and the earth trembled for about ten minutes. We thought we were going to die. My mother was angry with me for running upstairs and standing out in the open during the bombardment, afraid that I would be killed or injured.

The war was tough even before the German army invaded Hungary. Most of the Jewish men, including my father and Uncle Manó, were forced into the Hungarian army to do hard labour in the countryside and then many were shipped to the Soviet front. My uncle Manó, I later found out, had fought at the Don River in Russia and was taken prisoner. He never returned. Luckily, my father stayed in the country with his regiment, who wore civilian clothes and yellow armbands. He had occasional leaves, but sometimes we didn't see him for months, which meant that I was deprived of having a father for long periods of time. He was a stern man and we often didn't get along; nonetheless, it's hard on a young man to be without a father.

In the beginning of May, the Nazis designated a small area of Újpest as a Jewish ghetto and all 11,000 Jews had to move to houses in the ghetto within days. It took a week or so to fill the ghetto and then the Nazis closed it, putting soldiers outside to guard it and barricades up on all the streets that led out of it. We were trapped.

Fortunately we didn't have to move, as our house fell inside the ghetto area, but my sister, Ágnes, who was almost eighteen years old, was sent out of the ghetto to work and live in a forced labour textile factory in Újpest. We were allowed to leave the ghetto during the day and my mother visited Ágnes at the forced labour factory every other day, always bringing food. When the living conditions and lack of food started to worsen in the ghetto, our family discussed the possibility of escaping to Budapest, the only place in the country where things were better and where the Nazis had yet to establish a ghetto. But my mother wouldn't consider leaving my sister behind.

In the overcrowded ghetto, we secretly listened to BBC radio, which was illegal, hoping for some good news but the BBC only talked about the bombardment of German cities and targets. We never heard any news on the radio about Hungarian Jews or the transportation of Jews from the Hungarian countryside, cities and villages, but we did hear some people say that outside the ghetto, Jews were being taken away – nobody knew where or why. We didn't want to believe those stories. No one knew what would happen the next day.

Some time near the end of May 1944, my father found a gentile man who was willing to sell us three documents – his son's Christian birth certificate, school report card and Boy Scout membership card. The documents were appropriate for me because the boy was around my age. His name was József, or Józsi, a common name in Hungary, and his family name was Kovács, a typical Christian Hungarian name. So my new name was Józsi Kovács; I had to learn the name well and forget my real name. It took me days to learn my new name, where I was born and my new birthday. My father bought documents for my mother too, but she still didn't want to escape without my sister.

Although my mother wouldn't leave my sister, she was in favour of me escaping the ghetto. I think she could foresee the future and the danger of staying. I prepared a small suitcase of clothing and the next morning I said goodbye to my mother and kissed her. She was crying as I left the house to get the streetcar to Budapest. That was the last time I saw her.

That morning, my destination was not my school, as it had always been in the past, but an apartment in a small complex in Madách Square where Aunt Aranka, Uncle Frici and my cousins Vera and Tomàs were temporarily living with Frici's brother. Their family had left Újpest right after the Germans arrived, which had been easier for my uncle because he was blond with blue eyes and didn't look Jewish to the Germans. He could go outside without the yellow star and not worry too much about being caught.

I stayed with them for two or three weeks, talking about where to go and hide. By now, Polish Jews in Budapest who had escaped from other ghettos or camps were spreading the word of what was happening in the death camps in Poland and Austria. We all knew it was only a matter of time until the Nazis started to kill the Jews in Budapest, too. We discussed the possibility of escaping to the countryside to hide, but we knew that we could not all stay together. My aunt and uncle and Tomàs, who was only ten, had a place they could stay on a farm close to Budapest, but my cousin Vera, who was twelve, and I, now thirteen, had no place to go.

Then, one day in late June, my father came to tell us that he had found a place for me and Vera on a farm where he had a vine-yard, about 150 kilometres south of Budapest, close to the town of Soltvadkert. He had arranged it through our wholesale wine business on Bocskai Street in Budapest where Uncle Jenő, Aunt Lilian and cousin Iván lived. That house had a wine cellar full of large barrels of wine, most of which came from the Soltvadkert area. My father had bought the wine in wholesale quantities from a Jewish salesman who lived in Budapest with a Christian woman named Éva and it was her close relatives who had the farm near Soltvadkert. Her family – her parents, sister and eighteen-year-old brother – needed money because their wine production had been poor the previous year due to the weather, which was always a major factor in both the quality and quantity of wine. So my cousin Vera and I said goodbye to her parents and my father, and Éva took us by train to her father's farm.

The train trip there took almost eight hours and passed without incident. Éva's father, János bácsi (Uncle János, as we called him), was waiting for us at the station with his horse-drawn carriage to take us the rest of the way, about an hour's ride from the town. When we arrived, Éva introduced us to everyone as the two children from Budapest whose parents had sent them out of the capital because of the bombings. They believed the story. Only Uncle János knew that we were Jewish. Éva left the farm the next morning and took the train back to Budapest. We didn't see her again until late fall.

Uncle János had a typical Hungarian farm of about sixteen acres of land, including a five-acre vineyard. The rest of the land was planted with wheat and barley, and he also cultivated a vegetable garden around their small house with sweet red peppers and tomatoes. Pigs and chickens ran free in the garden. But most importantly, he had a few cows that provided milk to sell to the neighbours and for us.

I felt safe on the farm and in a few days got used to the lifestyle. I always loved nature, so it was easy for me to adapt. I also knew something about wine, although I had never cultivated or taken care of a vineyard before. Vera had a few difficulties getting used to the farm, but she was young, which often helps with adapting to a new way of life.

After a few days at the farm, Uncle János asked me if I was willing to come with him at dawn to cultivate the vineyard. He was a nice, calm and fair person in his mid-fifties and although he had some problems getting along with his son, who was lazy, we got along well and we both loved to wake up at dawn. I didn't know what we would do there but I said sure. He woke me the next morning, and I got ready quickly. As we walked to the vineyard, five minutes away, the sun was just starting to rise. When we arrived at the field, he gave me a garden hoe with a wide blade with a regular wooden handle and showed me how to remove weeds from between the grape plants. I was a fast learner and began right away. The soil was soft and tender so in the beginning it looked like easy work, but after three hours I was tired and hungry. Some stubborn weeds had to be pulled out by hand. At 8:00 a.m., János declared that it was time for breakfast so we went back to the house and ate homemade bread with *szalonna* (solid pork fat) covered with red paprika. We cut one slice of bread and a piece of ham fat with a sharp knife and ate them together, accompanied by coffee with milk. The breakfast was delicious – it was the first time in my life that I had eaten pork, since we kept kosher at home.

It was now the beginning of July and I continued to go with Uncle János every morning except Sundays to weed the grape vines. Being so occupied with the work on the farm, the days passed easily, but the nights were difficult. I missed my family, especially my mother. I thought about her a lot and had nightmares that the Nazis would somehow find me and kill me. I also had to look after Vera to ensure that she didn't tell anyone our secret. Many times, I reminded her of the danger we would be in if she talked too much. We had to be especially careful around János's son, who was openly pro-Nazi. Thankfully, he got called to the army a month after we arrived.

I knew little of what was happening on the war front or in the capital. We occasionally got letters from Éva but she didn't write details about the war or anything about my family except that they were all right. After a few weeks, Uncle János asked me to help him with other work too. He asked me to deliver milk every other day to the farmers who needed it. Uncle Janós knew that I could manage horses and a carriage because I had told him that was how I had delivered my father's wine to the stores. I had grown up with horses and I loved them. I think the horse is one of the most elegant and gracious of animals. When you talk to them, they often move their head up and down to show you whether they agree or disagree with what you're saying.

I had a dozen or more customers on my milk run and each one went well. I would knock on the door and they would come out with a bottle or container, tell me how much milk they wanted and chat with me a little. Sometimes they asked me where I was from and what my name was. Most of the customers were older women or men and weren't very interesting, except for a beautiful young woman named Maria. She was twenty years old and always nice to me and willing to talk. She told me that her husband was in the army and she was alone with no children. One morning when I arrived at her house to deliver the milk, she came out and, after we had said good morning, she suggested that I come into her house and stay a little while. I knew right away that she wanted a man to make love to her. I was thirteen years old but quite tall and muscular from my work in the fields and vineyards, so I looked fifteen or sixteen. I was also quite mature for my age – I had started dating girls at age nine or ten and my interest in them had grown every year. At thirteen, I felt ready for a sex life, and Maria was gorgeous and full of energy.

I stood there for a half-minute, thinking – I had to make a decision fast. I quickly came to the conclusion that it wasn't worth the risk: Hungary was a Catholic country where only Jewish boys were circumcised. She would have discovered that I was Jewish and might have told the local authorities, who would then arrest me. The country police could be brutally antisemitic and were helping the Nazis deport Jews to the camps. I was, of course, tempted to make love to that young woman and my decision was difficult, but I was in fear for my life. In the end, I told her, "I'm sorry but I'm very late with the deliveries today and cannot come in." For weeks, months and even years, I wondered whether I had made the right call. Now, I know I did. I wanted so badly to survive. I wanted to live and see my mother and family again. I believed in God deeply and I am sure that he helped me make that decision.

The weeks passed quickly and by the end of August the grapes started to ripen and we could eat them with bread and ham for breakfast every morning, which was a very tasty combination. Finally, toward the end of September, all the grapes were ripe and ready to harvest. The winemaking process, called a *szüret*, was a major festival involving three days of work, good food and lots of music and dancing. All the members of the family work during this time. The men did the heavy work, lifting baskets and transporting the grapes to the courtyard where the women cut the grapes from the plant. My expertise was once again useful to Uncle János – I knew most of the winemaking process from summers back home in Újpest. First, after crushing grapes in the machine, out comes the "must," the grape juice. Everybody drank that red, fresh and tasty grape juice, but if you drank too much of it, you got diarrhea. Everybody knew this, but it was hard to resist. Uncle János was the only one who didn't get diarrhea; he had to be well enough to command the harvest, which is the major event of the year. His income for the upcoming year depended upon it.

I was so busy with the harvest work and celebrations around it that I was exhausted by the end of the day. I slept so well for those three nights that I didn't think about the war at all. After the harvest there was not quite as much work in the fields and once again I started to miss my mother and the rest of my family.

In the second week of October, we got an unexpected visitor. János's daughter Éva arrived from Budapest with incredible news for us – we were going back home to the capital with her! We were ecstatic. Rumour had it that Miklós Horthy, the regent of Hungary, would announce that the country was going to pull out from the war with the help of the British army. My father wanted us to come back to Budapest right away, so Éva only stayed two more days and on the third day we were ready to go. We said goodbye to Éva's family at the farm and Uncle János got ready to take us to the train station in Soltvadkert. We all packed into the coach and arrived at the station about an hour later. We had plenty of food – much more than we needed because there was a shortage of food in Budapest. When I said goodbye to Uncle János and he kissed me, I felt I was losing a friend and an uncle. I never saw him again.

In normal peacetime the train trip took between five and six hours at most. But this was still wartime and the train was full of soldiers. It left the station early in the morning and moved slowly. But we were in high spirits and I certainly looked forward to seeing my family again. The three of us sat together in the middle of the train; fortunately, we were close to the exit door, which soon came in handy.

At noon we ate our lunches and relaxed as the train travelled along. During the afternoon, while many of the passengers were asleep, we suddenly heard the sound of an airplane. I looked out the window and saw an airplane coming straight at us at low altitude and after a minute I heard machine-gun fire from above. The planes swooped in fast, destroying the train engine and instantly killing the three engineers. When the train stopped, the passengers panicked and everybody tried to get off the train as fast as possible. The question was, where to go?

I grabbed Vera's hand and we ran from the train, Éva following closely behind. As we reached the bottom of the stairs I saw, just beside the exit door, a huge sewage pipe under the train. Some people were already hiding there, but most of the soldiers and passengers ran out into the open field. I didn't like that idea in case the planes came back. So I led Vera and Éva into the sewage pipe. The space was big enough to hide about fifteen to twenty people and we were the last three who could fit. My instincts had been right – the planes returned a few minutes later and shot at everybody in the open field. The pilots must have been targeting the soldiers and their rifles. I was at the opening of the pipe and could watch the attack. The machine gun noise was overpowering; it was a terrifying experience. The planes came back four times, with the whole attack lasting about eight or ten minutes. Seeing the low-flying planes, explosions, and people lying on the ground bloodied, injured and dying so close to us was horrifying.

That sewage pipe protected us and I thanked God for helping me make the right decision at that traumatic moment. I certainly hadn't had much time to think. We stayed on the train a day and a half, not moving, until a new engine was brought in and connected. On the evening of the third day we arrived at the large, old Eastern Railway Station in Budapest.

The Siege of Budapest

When we got off the train and out onto the main street we knew something strange was going on – the street was almost deserted and it was only 7:00 p.m. There were no taxis or transportation of any kind, so we started to walk to the apartment in Madách Square that we had left four months ago. On the way we saw a group of men in civilian clothes, armed with automatic weapons, marching on the other side of the street. They were Nyilaskeresztes, the Nyilas or Arrow Cross – the most feared members of the notorious right-wing Hungarian national socialist party – and Éva told us that they might have taken over Miklós Horthy's government.

We arrived at the apartment without being stopped by them only to have Aunt Aranka and Uncle Frici confirm our worst fears. The radio had announced that afternoon, October 15, that Horthy had been removed from office and the Arrow Cross Party was now in charge. We all knew what that meant – it was the beginning of the end for the Jews in Budapest. We had returned to Budapest at the worst possible time.

We stayed in the apartment for a week or so until Uncle Frici found a place that would offer us more protection from the Hungarian fascists – a bigger apartment for the five of us, that is, myself, Aunt Aranka, Uncle Frici and my cousins Tomàs and Vera. My father had been called away to the army again. The new location was on

Pannónia Street, one of the newest and best parts of the city. The apartment was huge, but we didn't have it all to ourselves – we only had one bedroom for all of us and would have to share the kitchen. My cousins and I only found out late that evening who would be living with us when four German officers, mostly middle-aged, entered the apartment with keys. I was shocked. My uncle explained to us in Hungarian that although these officers were in the Wehrmacht, the regular German army, they were against Hitler's war and would protect us. At this point, they knew that the war was lost; the Soviet army had already crossed the border into Hungary and was advancing every day.

We pretty much stayed inside the apartment. Being out on the streets was dangerous – Hungarian Arrow Cross soldiers or Nazis could catch us and kill us. Only my aunt and uncle, who spoke fluent German, went out for food. One evening the officers brought a few women to the apartment. They got drunk but were quite civil and not violent. They even gave us chocolate, although they sang and partied all night and I couldn't sleep.

We stayed with the officers for about three weeks. One evening, they told us they were leaving, that the Arrow Cross would be taking over the building and we should leave the apartment as soon as possible. By the next morning, it would already be too late. We packed quickly and went to another building on the same street that was under the protection of the Swedish legation. Uncle Frici had somehow been able to procure Swedish papers for the whole family and we were taken to the building's only available apartment. Later, Aunt Lili came back from a farm on the outskirts of the city and joined us. We had to go out to find food, which was now even more dangerous, so we had little to eat. We heard that the Arrow Cross were stopping men and forcing them to drop their pants to see if they were circumcised. If the Arrow Cross discovered that this person was a Jew, they took him to the Danube River and murdered him. The same was true if they discovered a Jewish woman.

It was raining lightly one morning at the end of November when I went to search for food. Without thinking, I put on a flat type of hat that, to my eyes, made me look more Jewish than I did without it and left the building. I had only walked about two hundred metres when suddenly two Arrow Cross soldiers with automatic rifles on their shoulders appeared from out of nowhere and asked for my papers. I had forgotten my Swedish papers but had all three Christian documents with me and took them out. After the soldiers had checked the documents, which were passable, one of them said, "Why would a thirteen-year-old Christian boy have three documents in his pocket?" "Something's not right," said the other. They told me to go into the building beside us – I could tell that they suspected I was a Jew. I knew that if I went into that building I would be lost; I was sure that I would be taken to the Danube and killed. So in a split second, I decided to run for my life. I grabbed all the documents out of the soldier's hand and bolted. Luckily, there were people on the street. I was close to the corner so I turned left almost right away and ran a whole block. At the next corner I turned left again and looked back to see if they were following me. When I didn't see them, I went into a building and climbed about twelve flights to the roof and stayed there until it was dark. I was on the roof without food or water for about six or seven hours. There were only Christians in that building and I was terrified that somebody would see me. I finally climbed down the stairs, looked carefully up and down the street and went home to the Swedish-protected house. I had been gone so long that Aunt Lili was really nervous. For the rest of the war, I never wore a hat again.

We stayed in the Swedish-protected building until we learned that the Arrow Cross had started grabbing people out of houses whether they were protected or not. Aunt Lili knew of an apartment that belonged to a Jewish family, friends of hers who had recently been forced to move to the Budapest ghetto that had been created at the end of November. About 30,000 people had been forced to move there. The next day, we left the Swedish building and went to the empty apartment, which was in a high-rise building on a main street, beside the movie theatre that only showed documentaries about the war. The apartment was on the sixth floor and the windows overlooked the street.

We started to familiarize ourselves with the space, searching for any kind of food. We were hungry and luckily found a ten-pound bag of white beans. There was also a bakery right across the street. Every morning there was a huge lineup and for a few pennies, each person could get about a hundred grams of bread. My aunt said that she would make a bean soup every day and each person would get one cup of soup per day. We had to ration the food because we had no idea how long the war would last. In the morning we had a plain piece of bread and in the evening, the bean soup. With only that amount of food, we were still always hungry, so we began to sleep a lot – it was the best way to ignore the hunger. We slept day and night.

We were only in that apartment for three weeks, until the last week of December 1944, when the Soviet army moved closer and their airplanes began dropping small, loud bombs that did lots of damage. We had to go down to the basement shelter and sleep there. The basement was long and dark, filled with eighty to ninety people, mostly women, children and old men. One of the old men, the superintendent of the building, was the Air Raid Commander. His job was to keep order in the building and to line up across the street for bread for everyone who lived there. When he suddenly got sick, I was asked to take his job. He took the wide armband from his right arm and put it on mine. I also wore a steel helmet, just like the soldiers on the front line. Part of my duty was to be sure that nobody but me went upstairs during air raids.

One morning I was standing in the thirty- to forty-foot-long bread line when airplanes began to strafe us with machine guns. Four or five people fell to the ground, badly injured or dead. Everybody ran. That day, I came back for the bread much later.

Another morning, I woke up early and as soon as it was light I got dressed, put my helmet on, placed my commander armband on and went up to the courtyard to get some fresh, cold air. I was in the courtyard when suddenly the gate of the building opened and two Arrow Cross soldiers came toward me. "Good morning, brother," they said. "We heard that this building has Jews hiding in it and you must tell us if that is true." I was shocked but didn't show it. "No! I am sure that no Jews are living here," I said firmly. "But if you want, I'll go down to the basement with you where everyone is." When they heard that they said, "We trust you. We won't bother. We'll try the other buildings to catch the Jews." So I said, "Goodbye, brothers," and they left.

The days passed slowly and the new year was close. Our food was almost gone. The Soviet army pressed hard – they were on the outskirts of the city and the bombings and shellings were frequent. There were lots of civilian casualties. We didn't know how long it would be until they took the city. We heard that the situation in the ghetto was awful, that there wasn't any food or heat and that lots of people were sick and dying. In the meantime, the Arrow Cross were still hunting down Jews and whenever they found them outside the ghetto, they forced them to the shore of the Danube River and shot them.

Early one morning in the second week of January 1945, I was awoken by a noise in the shelter. When I opened my eyes I saw a tall soldier with a light in one hand and a handgun in the other coming slowly toward me. He was followed by more soldiers, all belonging to the Soviet army. I recognized them right away and everyone in the shelter was happy and scared at the same time. I knew that at least we were finally free from persecution. I thought about my sister and my parents, wondering if they were alive.

The Soviet army had taken the city of Pest on January 17, 1945, but the Buda side, where the Germans had fortified the mountain with large cannons, remained in Nazi hands. A few days after taking the city of Pest, the Soviet army declared a three-day moratorium from regular law so that people could get to the stores, warehouses and factories to steal goods – we could go anywhere but houses or apartments. While people were searching for food, the army looked for luxury items like watches, clocks, jewellery and liquor. Some people found chocolate bars, hazelnuts, flour, sugar and other types of food in the warehouses. But I was only able to find perfumes and water colours. Before my eyes, one Soviet soldier collapsed after drinking from a bottle of perfume. This three-day rampage was unforgettable, and the looting continued long after.

One day as I was leaving the building to search for food, I saw two teenaged girls crying – they were sisters I knew from the shelter. I asked them why they were crying now, when the war was over for us, and they told me that they were Jewish and had just heard that their parents had been killed in a camp in Germany. I was shocked to find out that they had been hiding with us the whole time and I hadn't known they were Jewish.

We stayed in the apartment another few weeks and then Uncle Frici and Aunt Aranka asked me if I wanted to go back to their apartment in my grandparents' house to see if we could stay there. I did, and we left Pest for Újpest. We found the whole house – which hadn't been damaged by the bombardment – occupied by Soviet officers who were using it as a headquarters. My uncle asked them if we could stay and they told us that we could have one bedroom.

The next morning, my uncle and I both took our *tefillin* – phylacteries – and went to the living room to say our morning prayers. While we prayed, a Soviet officer entered the room. He had a gun in his belt and as he watched us he said in Russian, either "No good," or "Not right." I said to my uncle that I hoped that he wasn't an enemy of the Jews. The officer then repeated the same words and pointed to the *tefillin* on our heads. I got a little scared because we knew that part of the Soviet army that had entered Pest was a Ukrainian division, and that they were known for being antisemitic.

When the officer saw that we were scared, he said, "Shema Yisrael!" and we realized that he was Jewish, too. We were thrilled and he explained in Yiddish, which Uncle Frici spoke, what he had been trying to tell us – that prayers were not effective in wartime. He pointed to his gun and said that the only thing to do was use guns against the Nazis and kill them. He meant that resistance should be the most important thing for us, which I understood completely. Later on, I learned that the Polish Jews had had underground organizations that fought much harder against the Nazis than the Hungarians had.

I didn't stay in Újpest long. I decided to go back to Pest to stay with Aunt Lili in the apartment she had lived in before the Nazis invaded Budapest. My cousin Iván, who had also hidden on a farm not far from Pest, joined us. It was the beginning of February now and the winter was harsh and cold. There still wasn't enough food, the Germans on the Buda side were still shooting at us with their large cannons, and people were still dying.

One morning I was looking out the window and saw two dead horses in the middle of the street and many people – obviously very hungry – cutting chunks of horse meat to take home to eat. I loved horses like friends and although we were hungry, I couldn't do that.

We soon heard that there was more food in Szeged, a city 170 kilometres south of Pest, so the three of us decided to go there by train, the only transportation available. The second-largest city in Hungary at the time, Szeged had been liberated by the Soviets four months before Budapest. There had been a large Jewish population there before the war and the second-nicest synagogue in the country. Almost as soon as we arrived, I got a job there in a wholesale warehouse of bulk foods such as salt, flour and seeds of all kinds. The warehouse belonged to a Jewish man who had returned and found his store, warehouse and inventory intact – a rare situation in wartime. My job was to move the bags and look after the store when he was not in. He trusted me and Iván because we were Jewish. We got paid weekly with salt and matches, goods my aunt traded for big, fat, tasty geese. Before, in Budapest and Újpest, we couldn't even buy food with money, simply because there wasn't any. At last, after many, many months of hunger, we had good food and enough of it.

We stayed in Szeged for a couple of months, but by mid-April we wanted to go back to Budapest to find out what happened to my parents and my sister. I was hoping that I would find them home from the camps, but when we got back, they weren't there. I was sad and disappointed. I was fourteen years old, alone and desperately waiting for news. People were returning every day, looking starved and sick. I didn't lose hope. I trusted God.

And then, in the beginning of May 1945, some of my family arrived! My father and two of his brothers, Jenő and Sándor, and my sister, Ági, came back – they were very thin and in bad shape, but alive. My mother had not returned with them, but I still had hope she would come back soon. My cousin Tibor, Uncle Sándor's son, had died in the Bergen-Belsen concentration camp. He had already fallen ill when the Nazis deported my uncle, my father and him to the camp. At nineteen years old, Tibor had been the eldest cousin in our family. He had wanted to be a rabbi and had finished the first year of the rabbinical seminary in Budapest. I also learned that my paternal grandparents, who had moved to the city of Miskolc after Germany invaded Hungary, had been deported to Auschwitz some time in June 1944.

A few days after their homecoming, my father and my uncles told me the interesting story of Theresienstadt, the Czechoslovakian city of Terezin where in November 1941 the Germans created a model camp to showcase for the Red Cross, a place where Jews supposedly lived well despite being under Nazi occupation. In reality it was a ghetto and concentration camp. More than 33,000 prisoners died there from hunger, disease and maltreatment from the guards. Theresienstadt was also used as a transit camp for Jews en route to Auschwitz. There were about 60,000 inmates there, in barracks designed for 7,000 troops. By 1945, the Nazis had transported people who survived other camps to Theresienstadt; so many thousands of Jews were crowded there, including my father and his brothers. They had been taken to Theresienstadt from Bergen-Belsen in April 1945 and there were rumours in the camp that the Nazis planned to kill them all before the end of the war. One day, by chance, a man from Újpest recognized my father and asked him if he had seen his daughter, Ági – she was in the same camp. My father had had no idea that she was there. Ágnes had been sent there from a forced labour camp where she had been working in an armaments factory. The man took my father to my sister straight away and they cried with joy at seeing each other alive.

The date they reunited was April 21, 1945 – my fourteenth birthday.

The Aftermath

Soon after Ági returned she told me that before ending up at the armaments factory, she and my mother had been deported to Auschwitz together some time in July 1944. As soon as they climbed down from the train, my mother was immediately sent to the left, to her death. At that moment it hit me – my mother was never coming back. I had so much trouble coping with this reality that I was constantly exhausted, I lost weight and my heart began racing for no reason. I got worse week by week and I didn't know what was happening to me.

During the war I was scared and hungry – hunted, but mostly healthy. Now that the war was over, I got sick. I went to a doctor and after he examined me, he told my father and I that my thyroid was overworked, probably because of the anxieties I had suffered during the war. He was optimistic that with time and rest and fresh air my thyroid would work normally again.

At that time there were no drugs available for that kind of illness, so the doctors tried natural treatments. I was strong, but I sweated a lot and my heart frequently beat too fast. I was always hungry and very emotional. It was difficult for me to rest in the fresh air for hours, but I managed for a few weeks. Later, I found another cure for my illness when I discovered yoga and breathing exercises. Sometimes you can be your own best doctor. I began doing my own exercises five minutes at a time, three times a day and then increased to ten minutes. After only a few weeks, I felt better. I also opened the windows to get lots of fresh air and I began to swim again as soon as the pools reopened. It took about a year and a half for me to recover completely.

By May 1945 the war was officially over. We started to adjust and make plans for the future. We all agreed that we couldn't go back to live in the old house in Újpest; it held too many memories of my mother. My father leased an apartment in Pest on Damjanich Street, close to Heroes' Square, a well-known monument in the capital.

The old Jewish high school that I had attended before the war was still not open. Lots of teachers had died during the Holocaust. In Budapest, however, we had one of the best rabbinical schools in Europe, with such well-known professors as Professor Scheiber, who came from a famous rabbinical family. He was ready to open the school, but there weren't enough pupils. So he divided the building in half – one half remained the rabbinical seminary and the other became the *gimnázium* of Tarbut, a Hebrew-language high school – the first of its kind in Budapest. Before the war, there had been a Tarbut in Ungvár, a city in northeastern Hungary, where religious and Zionist Jews lived. Two brothers who had survived the Nazi camps and taught at that Tarbut *gimnázium* started operating the school in Budapest.

We had only three small classes but we had excellent teachers, including Professor Scheiber, whose books are well known. I always loved Hebrew and was good at it, so I went to the new school hoping to learn to speak and write modern Hebrew, the language spoken in Israel.

By the end of 1945, the Zionist movement was growing rapidly and all kinds of Zionist groups, from religious to socialist, had sprung up in Budapest. After the war and the Holocaust, Jewish youngsters wanted to belong somewhere and were looking for new ideals. The best place seemed to be the Zionist movement, with its hope for a new life, a new Jewish pride and the goal of founding the Jewish state of Israel. Thousands of Jewish boys and girls joined these groups.

Every day after school they danced, learned Hebrew songs, enjoyed being together and, most importantly, felt like they were home again. Many of them were, like me, without mothers, and some had lost both their mothers and fathers.

I decided to join Betar, an organization that was founded by Ze'ev Jabotinsky, a Russian Jew. Betar was strongly Zionist and claimed that Israel should be established on both sides of the River Jordan.

It was at a Zionist event that I saw Judit Katz for the first time. On that occasion, there were lots of girls and boys singing together, but I singled her out right away. I had flirted with lots of girls and went to the movies with a few, but when I saw Judit for the first time it felt different. Later, I knew that this was true love.

About a year after the war ended, my father told my sister and I that he was going to marry a "nice lady" by the name of Magda and that we would meet her soon. She was a ballerina, though I had never heard of her before. When my sister and I met her, a short woman with a nice-looking face, we were civil but stunned. She appeared to be the very opposite of our mother, but we couldn't really know her after only one meeting. My father married her a few weeks later and soon we started to feel her presence more and more. Unfortunately, my suspicion was 100 per cent right. She was twelve years younger than my father and very different from our mother. She was divorced and had never had children because of health problems.

Fortunately for my sister, she soon met and married a man named Endre and left home. I stayed, though I couldn't call it a home in the real meaning of the word. My father was a nervous type and Magda was hysterical and unbalanced, so they were often shouting and fighting. It was best to leave the house when they were fighting, but I couldn't always do that. Magda was kind to me sometimes, but she didn't really know what to do with me since she had never raised children; I was already a teenager and mature at age fifteen. She drove yet another wedge between me and my father, who was usually distant anyway.

I had a few close friends and we enjoyed things like swimming, gymnastics and going to dances but I felt like something was missing from my life. One day, I realized what it was. I was missing someone to love and someone who would love me, someone I could talk to freely and sincerely about my feelings, about my pain. A voice in my head told me: Go to that girl, Judit Katz. Go find her!

I didn't know where she lived or what school she attended, but I knew her girlfriend from one of the Mizrachi Zionist groups, so one night when I saw her girlfriend at a meeting, I asked her where I could find Judit. She told me that Judit swam in the famous Hotel Gellért pool on the Buda side of the city at a particular time.

When I first entered the pool area, which had a remarkable, old stone water fountain, I only saw Judit's girlfriend and asked her why Judit wasn't there. She replied, "Look down to the bottom of the pool. She's swimming underwater." I looked down and saw her so I jumped into the water, swam up to her under water and touched her leg. She was shocked that I had the temerity to touch her and she swam to the surface. I followed and when we were both on the surface, I said, "My name is George Stern and I want to get to know you." She didn't say a word then, but we talked after swimming a bit more. I waited for her in the lobby and made a date to see her again, this time without her girlfriend. And that is the way I met my wife.

We were young – Judit was fourteen and I was fifteen – but we were both mature. She came from a similar background to mine, an Orthodox Jewish family, although mine was more liberal. I would travel on Shabbat, for example, and she wouldn't, but we didn't have any issues with regard to our religious differences. She was a modest, intelligent, calm and balanced young girl and I felt good around her. At this point, I wasn't thinking about whether it was really love. It wasn't until a few years later that I knew that it had been love at first sight – a love that comes to a person once in a lifetime, if he or she is lucky.

Meanwhile, things got worse at home every day because of my

stepmother, Magda. As I tried to think of a way out, the solution suddenly came to me – I would make aliyah, immigrate to Israel – and just as I had that thought the door opened for me. It was the fall of 1946 and the Mizrachi Zionist group was looking for thirty teenagers under sixteen to make aliyah to pre-state Israel. My father was active in the Mizrachi organization and he was able to arrange for me to go. I was excited. My health was better and I began preparing for my journey.

I was looking forward to travelling by myself for the first time and I thought that I would be in pre-state Israel in a couple of weeks. I couldn't tell anybody that I was leaving because I was going with Bricha – the movement that organized the illegal mass exodus of Jews from across Eastern Europe to pre-state Israel. The Hungarian government prohibited leaving the country for Israel and since we didn't have exit visas the entire journey was planned secretly. We were told we would have to sneak across the border to Slovakia, but we didn't know exactly where we would end up. At that time, Czechoslovakia was sympathetic toward the establishment of the State of Israel and helped by supplying rifles and airplane parts. If the Hungarian guards had caught us at the border, however, they could have put us in jail and shut down that section of Bricha.

I prepared my backpack with clothes and things I wanted to take, and was told to hold onto it. A few days passed and then I got word to go to a place where a covered truck waited. I said goodbye to my sister, my father and Magda and left. I was happy, thinking that I would soon be in British Mandate Palestine where everybody spoke Hebrew and even the policemen were Jews. I had the feeling that my father didn't mind my leaving home for a few reasons, but mainly because Magda and I did not always get along. He had never had patience for me or my sister. He was all business, often distant, always stern. But he was my father and I loved him, even if it was difficult sometimes.

My group left Budapest one afternoon and at sundown we arrived at the crossing point, an open field close to the border where we waited for the guide to take us to the other side. He arrived just as it got dark and we were told to start walking. After one kilometre, we arrived at a river and the guide told us to take off our shoes and socks and cross it. The river was cold but not deep, maybe half a metre or so. I remember that we were not allowed to speak during the roughly ten-minute crossing.

We arrived safely in Czechoslovakian territory, relieved that we hadn't been caught by the Hungarian police. We put our socks and shoes back on, waited until the sun came up and then went by train to temporary housing in Nové Zámky, a town in southwestern Slovakia. We all shared a bungalow with a kitchen and a few rooms, the boys separated from the girls. People in Nové Zámky spoke both Czech and Hungarian, and the town had a nice synagogue. About five hundred Jews had returned there from the camps; before the war, more than two thousand Jews had lived in Nové Zámky.

The days and the weeks passed and we still didn't know when we would leave for British Mandate Palestine. After four weeks, I was bored with doing nothing and started thinking about returning to Budapest. At least in Budapest I could go anywhere and continue my schooling. I had left my friends behind and I missed Judit, too.

I wrote a letter to my father saying that I wanted to come back within a month. He replied that his first cousin Jenő, who was also in the wine export business, had a truck that came to Czechoslovakia every week and I could come back in it. He wrote the location and time where the truck would be and told me that the driver would know who I was. So when four more weeks passed and we still hadn't moved, I decided to exercise the plan.

On the morning when I knew the truck would be there, I packed my backpack and took the train to the bridge where the driver was supposed to arrive at midday on the Czechoslovakian side. The bridge crossed the Danube at Komárom, another Hungarian and Czech bilingual city about forty kilometres from Nové Zámky. I arrived before noon and waited until I saw a huge truck arrive. The driver recognized me and told me to get into the back, which was filled with empty wine barrels. I hid between barrels and we crossed into Hungary without any problems, arriving in Budapest in the afternoon. I later heard that my group eventually went to British Mandate Palestine many months later through Germany, and that they had ended up in an internment camp in Cyprus for a time.

For the next year and a half I went to school in the daytime and took evening courses to learn about radios and electricity. I always liked radios and as a small boy I had played with and built all kinds of electric cars, trains, small radios and even electric toys with little working lights. I also took night classes in English since most of the books in my radio courses were written in English.

Everything was the same at home, but I stayed away during the day and kept busy all evening, studying, swimming and dating girls. I went out with Judit too, and one day at the beginning of March 1947, around Purim, she asked me to come to her home to meet her family. Her mother, Blanka, and her father, Izidor, received me warmly and her sisters, Klara and Éva, were really nice. Judit later told me that I made a good impression on them.

Judit and I continued to date, often going to the nearby mountains to hike. I kissed her, but she was shy. I didn't want to do more than kiss her because I knew, and respected, that she was conservative and religious. Besides, there were many other girls older than me who were willing to make love without any guarantees from me.

Unfortunately, I didn't know Judit's mother long. Not long after I met her in the spring of 1947 she died suddenly one night at home. She had survived the Holocaust only to die two years later. The family was devastated. She was young, only forty-eight years old. I went to the shiva every evening to pray and I met the whole family – two aunts, one uncle and more relatives and friends. Among them was Aunt Margit, her mother's oldest sister, and Aunt Bözsi, her youngest sister. Margit was married but Bözsi was not. Two different personalities, just like Judit's sisters.

Just when a girl needs her mother the most, Judit was now, unfortunately, in the same situation that I was. The only thing that was a tiny comfort was that Judit was an independent girl.

Judit and I went together for a few more months and, for no reason at all, we stopped seeing each other. I think we had other priorities and little time to get together. I was busy with my studies and my friends and going out with other girls and trying to take life a little less seriously. I think, at age sixteen, I wasn't ready to get serious with Judit.

I enjoyed my teenage years, my school and girls, but I still wasn't happy at home. The months passed and in autumn of 1947 my life changed again. On the first day of October my sister gave birth to a boy, Tomàs Szántó. I was excited to be a first-time uncle at such a young age. I always loved children and I played with him often, as they lived within walking distance. Tomàs was an easy baby who rarely cried. I took lots of pictures of him and felt a special bond with him from the beginning.

Aliyah!

In the late summer of 1948, the government of Hungary gave permission for five hundred Jewish citizens chosen by Zionist organizations to immigrate to the new State of Israel with passports – the first legal aliyah from Hungary. Many more wanted to go, but, once again, through my father's work for Mizrachi, I had some influence and was told that I could go as long as I could get an exit visa. So I prepared once again to leave my country, my family – including my new nephew, Tomàs – and my friends.

At the end of October I received notice to go to a camp, at Csilléberc on the outskirts of Budapest, that would be the gathering place for our journey to Israel to begin. It proved to be quite comfortable – we all had rooms and beds in cottages. The next day, I was shocked to see Judit there and she was pretty surprised to see me too. Also part of the Mizrachi Zionist group, she had come with her aunt Bözsi. We hadn't seen each other for a few months and it was a welcome surprise.

We were in the camp about five or six days before heading to the train station in the south of the city, where we boarded a train that chugged across the southern part of Italy through Trieste and then to the small Yugoslavian port of Bakar, about eighty kilometres south of Trieste. It took us almost the whole day, but we arrived in daylight.

The train stopped near the shores of the Adriatic Sea – it was the first time in my life that I saw the sea, and it was remarkable.

That night, we slept on the train by the sea and in the morning, we were surprised to see that a much longer train had pulled up beside us. After a while, men, women, children and elderly people slowly climbed down from the train – many with bags on their backs and potato and onion plants in their hands. These people turned out to be four thousand Bulgarian Jews who had left their country with their dearest belongings and were now marching toward the ship, the *Kefalos*, an old Greek cargo ship that was to take us all to Israel. I suddenly had a picture in my mind of the Jews coming out of Egypt with their belongings, marching toward the Red Sea. The Bulgarians made an extraordinary sight, reminding me of those Jews so long ago.

The *Kefalos*, a three-deck, weathered and rusty ship weighing 3,800 tonnes, was quite big but not big enough for 4,500 people. The space was tightly packed; about five hundred people were crammed into the area I was in. The Bulgarians occupied 80 per cent of the ship but we had the best part of the vessel. None of this mattered, though – I just was happy that we were on our way to the Promised Land – to Israel.

Unlike Hungarian Jews, the Bulgarians had had Hebrew-language Jewish schools and spoke Hebrew well. I was the only one of our five hundred that could converse in Hebrew with them.

When everybody was on the boat, the *madrichim*, or leaders, closed the doors between the Bulgarians and the Hungarians. They didn't want them to mix because they couldn't communicate but since I spoke Hebrew, I was permitted to visit them. I got to know one Bulgarian family who had two small children and a beautiful daughter who was about fifteen years old. They liked me and always asked me to come to their side of the boat.

The other woman I got close to was a Hebrew school teacher who was between twenty-eight and thirty, and definitely single. She was pretty, warm and sexy and we communicated well in Hebrew. I hadn't ever had a sexual relationship with a woman like that. Because the air circulation under the deck was poor during the night, we slept together several times on the deck when the weather permitted, under the stars. Since it was November and quite cold, not many people slept on the deck. I had a warm sleeping bag that came in handy not only on the ship but also later in Israel.

Our meals on the ship were pretty terrible. We got only sardines and canned corned beef made in the US. But the worst thing was that although we had fresh water to drink, we didn't have any for bathing. We washed ourselves with salt water, which wasn't great.

After a few days, one of the engines broke down and the boat stopped in the middle of the ocean for a day and a half. I wasn't bored though, with so many people to talk to. I was also often entertained by the Bulgarian weddings, many of which happened on board because the Bulgarians believed that it was a mitzvah to be wed on the way to the Holy Land. One morning, the parents of the Bulgarian girl suggested I marry their daughter on the ship. They knew that if I didn't marry her they wouldn't see me after we landed. I was caught off guard, but adamantly refused. I was only seventeen and a half and didn't love her. I didn't visit that family again.

After a couple weeks, we got close to Israel and on the morning of November 28, we arrived in the Port of Haifa. Soon we began to disembark and our group, the Hungarians, were the first to go ashore. I was happy, excited and extremely moved to be on Israeli soil at last and I bent down and kissed the earth.

On the shore, we lined up to get fresh food, sandwiches, and milk or orange juice, and, after almost two weeks without fresh drinks and food, I felt better. Immigration officers sitting at a long table looked at our passports and asked questions. I was told I would be sent to an aliyah camp for civilians who were not between the ages of eighteen and forty-eight. The eighteen to forty-eight group were sent directly to an army camp. I was angry and told the officer, in Hebrew, that I had come to fight for the independence of Israel and that I had to go to the army. He asked my profession and when I told him that I was a radio technician, he said I could go to the army if I was prepared to sign a form saying that I had enlisted voluntarily. I promptly signed the form and was sent to one of the military buses waiting for new recruits. I was satisfied that I would finally be able to fight and help win the War of Independence against the Arab armies. The army needed more men and women because casualties were high and battles were still raging.

In the early afternoon I arrived at a former British military camp in the village of Beit Lid on the old highway to Haifa, fifteen kilometres from Netanya, where we would be selected for different army corps and issued uniforms. In the late afternoon, we got our uniforms and two blankets each and then were shown to our beds in a long, large tent. There were between eighty and one hundred people in the tent, most of whom were from Turkey. I put my blankets on my bed and slipped my backpack under it. It was a nice evening, still light, and I went for a walk and discovered that the camp was huge. I was gone for an hour and when I came back, my blankets had disappeared – they had been stolen. November nights in Israel can be cold, but I was shocked that Jews would steal from each other. I asked where my blankets were, but nobody responded. I told my sergeant, hoping to get new ones, but he said that the only way I could have blankets was to steal them back. So I did exactly that and went to sleep. It had been a long day. In the middle of the night I woke up to something dripping on me. It was rain – a surprisingly early rain for autumn in Israel. I got a little wet but it wasn't a big deal. The important thing was that I was in Israel, in the Jewish army, at long last.

At 7:00 a.m. we had the first *mizdar*, a sergeant's inspection, in full uniform, and were checked to see that we had dressed properly. That morning, we became real soldiers. After the inspection we got a medium-sized chocolate bar and a pack of cigarettes. I had never smoked before so I saved the cigarettes. Then we got permission to leave the camp for twenty-four hours to visit relatives or go to the city of our choice. My uncle Àrmin and aunt Sosanna lived in Tel Aviv on Bialik Street, right beside the old Tel Aviv city hall. I hadn't seen Uncle Àrmin for nine years, as he had left Hungary in 1939 when the war broke out. I took my bag and the chocolate and headed to Tel Aviv to see my Israeli family. I arrived at their house a few hours later and when I knocked, Sosanna, whom I had never met, opened the door. "You must be Gyuri!" she said, and kissed me. She invited me in and offered me food. I had the best "Welcome home" from an aunt I had never known. She was born in Poland and came to Israel with her mother and two brothers when she was fifteen. Their father had died before they left Poland.

After a while Uncle Àrmin, a dermatologist, finished his appointments and came out of his consultation room. Later I saw that it was full of cosmetic machinery from Switzerland. He welcomed me, saying, "Baruch Haba!" (Blessed is he who comes!) We kissed and they asked me to tell them about my adventures. I stayed at their home until the next morning, sleeping on the floor because their apartment was small. Their two daughters, Nurit, who was six-and-a-half, and Nizza, who was one-and-a-half, shared one room. Nizza was difficult to feed because she refused to swallow anything, but she was cute.

In the morning I left and went to explore Tel Aviv, the sea and the beaches, which were not far from my uncle's apartment. Tel Aviv in 1948 was quite small and most of the stores were on Allenby Street and Ben Yehuda Street. There was only one bigger building on the beach and that was the temporary Knesset, the Parliament, which later became the country's first opera house. Restaurants and one-storey banquet halls lined the shore north of the Knesset and at the end of the block was the most famous restaurant in Tel-Aviv, Café Piltz, which had dancing in the evening to the Duci and Carlo Band. Three of my father's cousins whom I had never met were in this four-person ensemble. Duci Stern was his first cousin and the other two men were husbands of his two other cousins, Manci and Lili. They lived in Zagreb before the war and played on Radio Belgrade after the war. After touring the city I hitchhiked back to my camp in military cars.

On my third day in Israel, during morning inspection, we again received one pack of cigarettes and one chocolate bar. On the fourth day they started assigning people, sending them to different corps or brigades. I was sent to the Signal Corps, in Hebrew, the Heyl Hakesher. One morning, after a week in the camp, a Jeep came to pick up me and a few other soldiers to take us to the outskirts of Tel Aviv to a place referred to simply as the *kiriyot*, the suburbs. Here, we were housed in a camp that had previously belonged to the British government that had small buildings instead of tents, which was much more comfortable than the previous camp.

I arrived at the headquarters of the Signal Corps and gathered around the dinner table with the other twenty-five officers. The next day at breakfast I met two Czechoslovakian soldiers, Egon and Ervin, who were telephone and telegraph repair technicians. They were born in the city of Košice, now part of eastern Slovakia, where Hungarian had been spoken since World War I, so we could speak to each other in Hungarian and soon became close friends. On the table was good food and margarine, which I had never eaten in Hungary, and plenty of olives. I had also never eaten olives before and when I tried one it was bitter and I couldn't swallow it.

There was a food shortage in the country at that time and civilians used food stamps, which they had to pay for, to buy essentials. There were shortages of sugar, oil, olives, margarine and eggs. When I next got a twenty-four-hour leave from the army, I visited my family and told Aunt Sosanna about the olives and the margarine. She asked me to bring as much as I could because they loved olives and needed margarine.

We stayed at the headquarters for about five days and then, as part of our training for the Signal Corps, we were sent to an intensive eight-day session at an officers' training camp to learn to use rifles, automatic pistols, machine guns and hand grenades. The training was dangerous, conducted with real bullets. At the end of the course, we all knew how to shoot and how to use the rest of the weapons.

We came back to headquarters and the next day a few of us were sent to the 5th Brigade, the tank headquarters at Bilu, a few kilometres south of the city of Rehovot. My job was to establish and look after the workshop for all the radio equipment, all of which was old, as were the tanks and the cars. I was stationed in a small building that contained the office, the laboratory and the separate bedrooms for female and male soldiers. Eight people, two women and six men, worked there. The women worked in the office and the supply warehouse. One female soldier, whose name I can't remember, was originally from Yemen. She was about twenty-three years old and was a sergeant. The other girl, Malka, was a Sabra – a native-born Israeli – and she was around eighteen years old. They had been in the army since the beginning of the 1948 Arab-Israeli war. They both flirted with me and I got close to the young Yemenite woman. She had a bit of a temper but she was kind. We connected on a physical level, but I didn't fall in love with her.

After a week or so, near the end of December, I was sent along with an armoured car column to the last battlefield in the Negev desert called the Faluja pocket, where fierce battles had raged between us and the invading Egyptian army, headed by Abdel Nasser, who later became president of Egypt. At first, the Egyptian forces took part of the Negev, but we eventually succeeded in liberating it and our army encircled the Egyptian army until February 1949.

We had suffered a lot of casualties but I returned safely from my first battle experience at the front, which was one of the last battles for the independence of Israel. We won the war and Israel was saved. Finally, we had a country.

Judit

By the spring of 1949, I had been in Israel for five or six months. The war and the excitement of a new country made it a busy time in the army. I celebrated my first Passover seder at Uncle Àrmin's home, which reminded me of the seder in my grandfather Fülöp Stern's home. My cousin Iván joined us. He had journeyed to Israel ten months before me from the displaced persons camps in Europe and had also spent time in an internment camp in Cyprus.

All this time, I hadn't heard anything from Judit, but I thought about her often and missed her. I knew that one day I would meet her again. When I had come back from the war, the Yemenite sergeant I had dated earlier was happy to see me and later asked me to marry her; I said no and a few months later I stopped going out with her. Malka, the other female soldier, asked me to go out with her and since I was now single, I agreed. Malka was born in Tel Aviv. She told me that her father was rich and when we went to Tel Aviv to the Cinema Mugrabi, the biggest in the city, she told me that her father owned that theatre and several others. I didn't understand why she told me all this until later, when she let me know she'd be happy to be my wife, and that I too would be rich. Only one thing was missing – I didn't love her. I couldn't marry anybody I didn't love. By the summer, I stopped going out with her, too.

I got leave from the army almost every Saturday and went to Uncle

Àrmin's home. One Saturday afternoon in the fall I went for a walk along Allenby Street and saw somebody familiar walking toward me. It was Judit! We hadn't seen each other in almost eleven months. Our happiness at meeting again was tremendous. We walked and talked all afternoon, sharing stories about what had happened to us. After we arrived in Israel, Judit and her aunt went to an immigration camp in Pardes-Hanna. Now, she was in a girls' school in Jerusalem and her uncle Yakov Katz, a professor, had arranged for her to stay at the school. Her aunt Bözsi was in a seminary in Jaffa.

A few weeks after our encounter I went to visit Judit at her school in Jerusalem and she was very pleased to see me. It was almost winter and was quite cool. We went for a walk and Judit showed me many houses that had been bombed by the Jordanian army during the 1948 war. I was in uniform and had one more year to serve. At that time, men had to serve two-year terms.

Two months later, in the middle of winter in early 1950, I visited her again. Judit had learned Hebrew quickly and spoke it well. She was working with children at the Ra'anana school and wanted to be a kindergarten teacher. It was dark when I arrived at her school and I was wet from head to toe from a heavy winter rain, but I was excited to see her. We stayed in her room all evening while my clothes dried. I had to go back to my camp that same night but we had a lovely evening together, an evening we've never forgotten, and I returned to camp at midnight.

The next few weeks she was often on my mind. I missed her, so I went to see her again. She invited me to the wedding of one of her cousins in the city of Bnei Brak the following week, just outside of Tel Aviv; she wanted her family in Israel to get to know me. Judit, to this day, loves and keeps family very close. I went to the wedding, where there were about fifty people, and she introduced me as her boyfriend. I sat among her cousins and when I wasn't looking, they added vodka and liqueurs of all kinds to my drinks. I had a great time, but I got drunk, very drunk. I had never been drunk before. I talked a lot and much of it was probably nonsense. The wedding finished late at night and the cousins took me to the bus station. Because I had the next day off, I went to Uncle Àrmin's house. I arrived after midnight and found my cousin Iván home, too. Since I was singing quite loudly, he could tell that I was drunk, so he put me to bed and tried to calm me down. The next morning I had a hangover and remembered little of what had happened the night before. Iván told me as much as he could. So, the first time Judit's family met me, I had acted like a drunkard.

The next time I went to visit Judit, we decided to get married when I completed my army service in eight months. I wanted to marry her right away, but she said she wanted her husband to be home, not in the army, and would gladly wait another year or so.

At the 1950 Pesach seder in my uncle's house, Judit was invited as my fiancée. When we had gotten engaged, I told my two best friends, Egon and Ervin, the news. They asked to meet Judit, so I arranged a get-together at a well-known café in Tel Aviv. I was sitting there with Judit when they arrived and I introduced her, in Hebrew, as my fiancée. I saw by the looks on their faces that they were surprised. When Judit, who was dark-skinned with black hair, went to the ladies' room they asked me, "Are you crazy, marrying a Yemenite girl?" Yemenites were darker skinned than many of us and in those days mixed marriages were frowned on by almost everyone. My friends were shocked to think I was going to marry a person of colour. I answered, "Why shouldn't I?" But when she came back, I signalled her to speak Hungarian and my friends almost fell out of their chairs. I jokingly told them that Judit was a Yemenite girl born in Budapest.

My discharge from the army seemed far away to me and I got bored. The war had been over for more than a year and I was counting the weeks until I could be out. My superiors wanted me to join the permanent army for at least five more years with an officer's degree, but I wanted freedom. Though I had wanted to fight for Israel's survival and be part of the founding of the nation, I didn't like army life. Finally, after two years of service, the time came for me to be discharged. I was as happy to leave as I had been to enlist. I went to live with Uncle Jenő and Aunt Lili, who had been in Israel since 1949. They had a two-bedroom apartment in Ramat Gan, a growing city on the outskirts of Tel Aviv. I had one bedroom to myself. I got along well with Aunt Lili, with whom I had survived part of the Holocaust.

I started searching for a job in my profession right away. Judit and I were to be married and I needed money. I found a job in the post office, which needed radio and radar technicians to build communication links with the rest of the country. First, I worked in Tel Aviv in the post office's main lab with two engineers, one from England and one from Poland. They designed the equipment and I built it. The work was too easy, so I asked my boss to arrange a more interesting job with a better salary but it wasn't going to happen. They liked me just where I was. A few months later, in the spring of 1951, the post office needed a team to set up the first mobile post office in Be'er Sheva, complete with a radio communication system and cars to deliver mail and parcels to the surrounding kibbutzim – collective farms – and communities. All the cars needed to be equipped with radios – the same work that I had done in the army in tanks and armoured cars. I put together a three-man team and went to Be'er Sheva, where we got a bungalow. Be'er Sheva was a small Arab-Bedouin village, a kind of market centre of the Negev.

We put up the Israeli flag and started to work. After two weeks, the first fully equipped postal cars started deliveries and the office also sent telegrams and provided phone service. We were proud to be the first to set up the communications system, which the Negev population depended on. My team returned to Tel Aviv and were transferred to post office headquarters in Tel Aviv, and another team stayed in Be'er Sheva permanently to run the post office.

I soon received a letter from my father saying that he was glad that I was going to be married, and he asked us to wait until he and Magda could come to Israel, which would be in the summer. Judit and I decided that we would. They arrived in early summer and rented an apartment in Giv'atayim, a suburb of Tel Aviv, but I stayed with my uncle and aunt until my marriage.

Judit and I decided to get married on August 16, 1951. We chose a nice restaurant in Ramat Gan with a garden terrace and started to plan our wedding. First we went to the rabbinic office because in Israel, that is the official government office to approve a marriage. Two or three rabbis checked our birth certificates and asked me if I was a *cohen* – a member of the tribe of *Cohanim* (the Priests). Judit's surname, Katz, indicates that she is a daughter of a *cohen*, but I am an Israel, meaning that I am from the tribe of Israel. For the next half hour, the rabbis tried to convince Judit that she had to marry a *cohen*, not an Israel. She told them, "I love him, as Israel as he is, and I want to marry only him." The rabbis gave up and gave us a paper that would allow us food stamps for the wedding party. The next day we picked up the stamps and then went to the store to buy the food for the party; to our surprise, though, the stores didn't have most of the foods we needed.

Israel had been officially undergoing *Tzena*, austerity measures, since 1949, due to a shortage of food and other goods. The measures were imposed by prime minister David Ben-Gurion, who appointed politician Dov Yosef to be minister of rationing and supply. We could only get essential foods such as oil, sugar, eggs, wheat and meat, on a point system or with food stamps. Sometimes, they weren't available at all. The only thing the country had enough of was frozen fish, mainly fillet of sole and cod.

I told Aunt Sosanna about our problem and she said that she would buy the food from her own store and that other retailers were charging way too much. She bought the ingredients to make cakes and other delicacies, but the only fruits available in Tel Aviv were oranges and grapefruit, which weren't festive enough for a wedding. At this point, Uncle Jenő came to the rescue. He had a good friend on a *moshav* – a farm – about forty minutes by car where grapes were grown, and he would be willing to give us some if we picked them ourselves. In Israel, grapes ripened in August. So to have grapes fresh from the field we decided to go with Iván, who had a car, to pick the grapes early in the morning on the day of the wedding. We managed to collect enough grapes and be back before noon, well in time for the evening ceremony. Judit's aunt Bözsi also helped us organize the celebration.

The chuppah, the traditional wedding canopy, was simple and under the open sky. We didn't have a cantor, only a rabbi, and there were about eighty guests. We were all excited, especially me – that is my natural way. And on August 16, 1951, at 7:30 p.m., Judit and I said, "Yes." The sweet table was beautiful; the grapes were delicious; the music was lively and the party went until 11:30 p.m. We were very much in love and extremely happy to be married.

After an overnight honeymoon in a hotel, we moved to our new home, a small house that I had rented in a new suburb called Shikun Vatikim, about five or six kilometres from Netanya. The area, geared toward new immigrants, was comprised of small, one-bedroom bungalows, each with a piece of land. I rented the house from Duci Stern, my father's cousin whom I mentioned earlier. Duci had been lucky to get the house from the government and he now rented an apartment in Tel Aviv.

The move was easy for me and Judit because we had almost nothing aside from some clothes. I had money saved to buy a few chairs, some plates to eat on and a small table. Uncle Àrmin had given us an iron bed as a wedding gift and we got a mattress from Uncle Jenő a few days later. Our house was a tiny 450 square feet and had one bathroom. We used oil lamps, as neither the house nor the village had electricity. Only the main streets of the village were paved. Everything else was sand – the whole suburb was a big city of sand, but we were content. We had each other.

There was only one bus that went to Netanya every four hours and the village didn't have any stores. The milkman came in the morning and the iceman came once a day, but we never knew when. At first, we didn't have an icebox, so we didn't need ice. However, we soon had to buy one because in the hot climate, food only stayed fresh for a few hours. As newlyweds, we were entitled to a government stamp to buy an icebox. Unfortunately, there weren't any near us left to buy, even if you had stamps. Luckily, Aunt Sosanna's stepfather sold iceboxes and after four weeks we were able to buy a small one. It cost four-months' salary but at least food wouldn't spoil anymore – or so we thought. Now the problem was that we often couldn't get ice. Either the iceman didn't come, or he came when we were out working; sometimes even when we rushed to the main street to his carriage, he was already sold out. The distance from our house to the main street was half a kilometre but I was glad to carry that half a block of ice, which was all that we were allowed. It was heavy and the weather was hot, but we didn't complain. We were satisfied with that half block of ice and we were young, in love, and thinking about building a family.

When we moved to Shikun Vatikim I quit my job in the post office. It didn't pay well and it was too much travel. So Judit and I were both looking for work. We needed money to buy the many things we didn't have. I soon found work on the other side of the main highway in Beit Yitzhak, an agricultural village founded by German Jews. The soil there grew watermelons and white radishes, which Polish and Russian Jews love to eat with their matzah ball or chicken soup all year round. We Hungarians sometimes ate white radishes, but only on Jewish holidays. I got work in the watermelon fields from 6:30 a.m. until 2:00 p.m. There was no bus so I walked there, which took twenty minutes. I loved the work, the fresh air and watching the melons grow bigger every day, but the job didn't pay enough, so I only worked there for five months.

Then, I heard that I could get double the pay making cement blocks for house construction. I found a Yemenite village where the government was building a school and they needed block makers. The village was about a twenty-minute car ride away, so not too far, and I could hitchhike there easily. I worked from 6:00 a.m. to 1:00

p.m. The blocks were heavy and I had to carry them quite a distance to lay them down to dry for a day so they could harden. I was strong but it was hard work. My fingers and hands got so stiff and strong from the work that once, when I was drinking from a glass, it broke in my hands. After that, I drank from heavy china cups.

We were soon thrilled to learn that Judit was pregnant. She had been attending a six-month course to learn to be a kindergarten teacher and had to travel there every day on the bus. After the course, she got a job as head of the kindergarten in one of the Jewish-Tunisian immigrant villages near the Jordanian border. When she got the job, she was about three months pregnant.

In the village I worked in, Jewish-Yemenite immigrants grew vegetables and garlic. One day when we finished work, a woman invited me and the other two men I worked with to her house for lunch. My colleagues refused her offer, but I was curious to see how they lived and what they ate. When I got inside her house I almost fainted from the strong smell of garlic. The woman showed me that she was cooking a mass of raw garlic, water and flour. The smell was so heavy that I thanked her and rushed out into the fresh air. I heard once that Yemenite Jews are rarely ill and I think their good health can be attributed to their garlic consumption.

My cement work lasted only a few summer months and between 1952 and 1954 unemployment was high in Israel. I went to the employment office in Netanya and asked for work – any work or, better yet, work in my profession. The officer told me that there might be jobs in the Schnapp battery-manufacturing company, in an area close to where I lived. He told me to go to the factory and to bring back a letter of confirmation from them if they hired me. There was only a field between the factory and our house, so it was just a ten-minute walk and I went there right away. The manager, a Czech Jew, interviewed me. He then called in the engineer and owner, Mr. Schnapp, a German Jew who had founded the factory a few years before in Haifa and then moved it to bigger quarters in Netanya.

Mr. Schnapp asked me about basic electronics and my background. He was impressed and hired me on the condition that I work Saturdays, with double pay, since batteries need to be watched when they are in the electric-circuit filling process. I took the job. The pay was all right and I needed the money. I received the letter of employment and the next morning I rushed to the employment office to obtain the mandatory approval from the government and the union. I thought everything would be fine but when I gave the official the letter, he told me that I had to come back a few days later. I figured out that he wanted to give my job to somebody else. I went ballistic and took his office table and lifted it up, ready to throw it in his face. I told him if he didn't sign my letter and give me the approval, I would break his face with the table. I guess I was a bit desperate for the job. He was terrified and quickly gave me permission to work in the factory. I put the table back on the ground and left. I had what I wanted. I had the job.

I started work the next morning in a part of the factory called the electric charge room. It was a large area and I was the boss; nobody gave me orders. I worked with three Arab men, two Christians and a Muslim. They had been the first employees in Haifa and I got along well with them. Schnapp was bossy and liked to order people around, but he was decent to me. He came to my room once a day to oversee the operation, but I worked efficiently and not one battery spoiled. Thirty-five people worked in the factory, and twice a day we were each given a half litre of milk to neutralize the effect of the gases that polluted the factory. During the first week, I kept finding holes in the seat of my pants. I couldn't understand why until I discovered I was wiping the battery acid off my hands on my pants and the acid was eating through them. I learned to remember to clean my hands on a cloth.

Every day after work, I worked in the garden around our house. We had quite a big lot but the soil was sandy. I raised chickens and a duck because Judit liked ducks. I grew peanuts, which flourished in the sandy soil, and planted tomatoes, which were my favourite. They also grew well in the sand, but needed water every day. I had always loved growing vegetables and enjoyed working in the fields, so much so that after we married I had wanted to live in a farm community and have six or ten children. Judit was cool to the idea, but was willing to go along with it. I had looked into a farming village but it cost four to five thousand dollars to establish a farm, which at that time was quite a lot of money. I tried to raise the cash everywhere I could – banks, government, family, my father – but nobody wanted to either give or loan me money for a farm. I was especially disappointed by both my father's and the government's refusal – disappointed in the government because I was just out of military service and a penniless soldier, and my father because he should have loaned me the money he had inherited from my mother's property. I actually should have gotten half of that money, which would have helped me start a new life on the farm. In the end, I had had no choice but to drop the idea.

Judit worked almost until the ninth month of her pregnancy. It was difficult for Judit to continue working, especially in summer. The weeks passed and we waited every day for our first child to be born. A few weeks before she was due I decided to grow a moustache to look older. I was almost twenty-two and I wanted to be more serious-looking as a father.

Because there was no hospital in Netanya, Uncle Àrmin arranged for Judit to go to the Tel Aviv Hadassah hospital, the best in the country. I took her to stay in my uncle and aunt's house, which was close to the hospital. She stayed with them for a few days while I worked in the factory, always anxious for news. Every day, I asked the manager in the office if I had received a phone call from Tel Aviv, in case he forgot to tell me. He was a friend, too, so he calmed me down and told me that he would not forget to tell me the moment he got the call. Those few days were the longest and most anxious time of my life. Finally, one morning around noon, I got the call from my uncle. He told me the fabulous news – I had a son, a healthy son, and Judit was doing fine. I was thrilled and excited and the whole factory stopped for ten minutes to give me best wishes. I got two days off work and I went to change and then left for Tel Aviv to see my wife and brand new son. Jochanan Pinchas Stern, who we came to call Paul, was born on January 12, 1953, at 11:45 a.m.

I arrived at the hospital in the early afternoon and I went straight to see Judit. She looked great. She was in a room with eight or ten other women – most of them were Sephardic Jewish mothers who thought, because of Judit's dark skin and hair, that she too was Sephardic. When I visited, most of the Sephardic women were shocked to see that Judit's husband was a white-skinned, blond Ashkenazi.

Then the nurses brought in my son. Paul was quiet and I was afraid to hold him at first, so I gave him a kiss instead. Judit stayed in the hospital seven days until we had the *brit milah* there, arranged by my uncle. I was very excited on the morning of the *brit* and to look nice I decided to trim my moustache. I unfortunately cut too much off one side so I had to shave the whole thing off. That was the end of my first moustache.

The *brit milah* went smoothly except that I almost fainted when I saw my son bleed and cry. But he soon fell asleep and after the ceremony the three of us went home as a happy family. I had already bought a bed for Paul, which we placed in our one bedroom. Paul was a good eater and slept quietly through the night. He was so quiet that sometimes I woke up in the middle of the night to check that he was alive and well. Judit wasn't producing enough milk so I fed Paul with formula from a bottle. He always finished it and wanted more, so I gave him another half bottle. He loved to eat and he grew nicely.

We had saved some money and started to look for a small condominium in Tel Aviv. We had only enough money for a down payment, but we finally found one in a new five-storey building, although it didn't have an elevator. It was on the main street in the best location in town, across from the bus station. On the first floor were offices and stores and there was a new movie theatre in the basement. We negotiated the price of the apartment down to six thousand Israeli pounds – one thousand down and twenty monthly payments of 250 pounds, which was about Judit's salary from the government.

Paul was one and a half years old when we moved to the apartment in late summer 1954. The apartment was more spacious than our rental had been. We had two rooms, a larger bathroom, electricity and, most importantly, the apartment was ours. I was always against renting because you save money if, instead of paying rent, you pay off your mortgage or loans.

After we moved to the apartment I felt that the factory job wasn't paying enough. And it bothered me that I wasn't working in my radio profession, so I began looking for a job in my field. I discovered that the air force was looking for radar technicians in a location an hour and a half from Tel Aviv and I applied there. After an examination, I was hired by the Israeli Air Force's central laboratory for repairs and research to repair airplane radios. Both my salary and working conditions improved. Instead of tank radios, which I had worked on during the war, I repaired more complicated communication systems. I preferred this because I had to learn new things all the time. I woke up every morning at 5:00 a.m., took the bus at 6:00 a.m. and began work at 7:30 a.m. I always loved to wake up early, something I inherited from my grandmother Bertha, who had always woken up with the chickens.

I also started a repair business at home for regular radios. I put a sign downstairs that said Stern Radio Repairs and Renewal and at night I fixed lots of radios; the whole city had only three radio shops, including mine. It was difficult to buy a new radio because the country had no radio factory yet.

I earned decent money from the repairs – sometimes more than my salary from the air force – but I worked many nights until 1:00 or 2:00 a.m. We needed more money now, with a son to take care of, and we had the apartment to pay for. On top of that, we always seemed to need something new.

Two neighbours moved in soon after us – one family beside us and another across from us. Living beside us in the corner apartment were Aron, an army officer, and his French-Jewish wife, Rivka, who lost her parents in the war. Their daughter was about Paul's age. We got along well and became close friends. Aron often got a Jeep or car from the army and sometimes we toured the country together.

Across from us was another nice young couple and their two boys, Zvika and Benjamin. The man's name was Avram but we called him Vimi. He was born in the US and his wife, Chana, was a Sabra, born in Afula, a city in northern Israel. Her parents were Hungarian. Avram was over six feet tall and he was a good handyman; he did most of the work around the house. We three couples became close friends and we were all ready to help each other in any way. Our friendship was something special and has continued until today.

One day, Aron came up with the idea of installing a crane on our balconies so that we could put heavy stuff in a basket and pull it up to our apartments. It was difficult to carry blocks of ice or things like large watermelons (which we all loved, especially our son) up five flights of stairs. We bought the equipment and installed two cranes – one for each of us. Vimi used our crane because we couldn't install one on their side of the apartment. When we tested it the first time it worked very well. We had a party that night to celebrate.

Our children were also good friends. Zvika was almost the same age as Paul, and Benjamin was about two and a half years older. Zvika was a good child, but he seemed to live to beat Paul up, and Paul was a quiet boy who was never violent. He had no fighting spirit. He ran away most of the time but when he was beaten up he would complain to me. I felt that I had to do something to teach Paul to defend himself so one weekend morning I told Zvika to beat Paul up until he looked like he was in a bit of pain. I made sure I was there when the beating happened, to see that no serious damage occurred. And Zvika beat Paul until he got mad and started seriously fighting back. After that, Paul never ran away and Zvika never beat him again. My son had learned to defend himself.

Waves of Change

One day at the beginning of October 1956, I got a call to go to my army unit headquarters in Bilu immediately. I assumed that this was the usual call for *miluim*, two to three weeks of annual army reserve duty with salary to keep you in shape and up to date with army tactics. When I met up with my team in Bilu the next day, we were given regular army uniforms and equipment and started checking the tank radios to make sure they were in perfect operating condition. At first, I thought that this was routine work, but when so many tanks came and went I began to suspect that something else was going on. I was right – after three and a half weeks of constant work, we learned that war had broken out with Egypt due to a conflict over the Suez Canal and we were going to the Sinai Desert. The next day, after most of the tank division had left, we received orders to go south to the Sinai.

We travelled by Jeep and armoured car; it took almost a day to get there. Our tank division quickly broke through the Egyptian defenses and we advanced toward the Suez Canal. Travelling in a large, enclosed truck that contained a complete mobile repair shop, we met up with our tanks again in a small Egyptian village in the middle of the desert. By the time we got there, the village was empty. Once it had been taken, the entire population had fled. Lots of Egyptian soldiers lay dead in the street.

The next day we continued to advance and by evening we arrived at a junction about twenty-five kilometres from the Suez Canal. At that point, we were ordered to stop and wait. The night was dark, moonless. At 3:00 a.m. we were woken up and I was ordered to stay outside with my rifle and guard my regiment. There were two or three of us and we walked around cautiously. It was cold and the time passed slowly; the night seemed endless. At 5:30 a.m. the sun rose and I suddenly noticed a large number of dead Egyptian soldiers on the sides of the road. I had been walking among them the whole night without knowing it. I wasn't scared – they were all dead – but it was a strange feeling to have been walking for hours around corpses.

In the afternoon, my friend, the captain of my Signal Corps and a daredevil type, asked me and two other soldiers if we wanted to join him on a trip to the canal in his Jeep. I asked, "When?" and he told me, "Now, this afternoon." I thought for a moment and said, "No, not in the daylight." A few Israeli guys alone in the desert were easy targets and we didn't know where the retreating Egyptian army was. "I don't want to die," I told him. "I have a wife and small boy at home awaiting my homecoming." But I agreed to go with him that night for a swim in the canal. When it was dark, we drove slowly for an hour, checking to see if the enemy was on the horizon. All was quiet and vacant at the canal; we were the only ones there. We swam for half an hour or more, lay on the shore a couple of hours and then returned to our regiment in the middle of the night. It felt like the longest trip I ever took. We swore not to tell anyone; the trip was against orders and we could've been sent to jail.

During the war, I was terrified of the mines that the Egyptian army had scattered in the desert. We had advanced so quickly that we hadn't had enough time to clear the mines. I saw our cars and army trucks hit mines and blow up, and there were a lot of casualties. Those mines were the only thing I feared, but with God's help, I made it through. At the beginning of November, the Suez Crisis had diminished. I stayed in the army for another month and a half to make sure the radio equipment in the tanks was in good order. Then, after two and a half months of service, I was discharged.

Judit didn't know I was coming home, but she told me later that just before I got there, Paul said to her, "Mom, my daddy is coming. He's here." He had not even seen me yet – I was just at the gate of the building, but his sixth sense told him I was home. Judit said, "No, Paul, he is not home yet, but he will be any day." A few minutes later I knocked on the door and when Paul opened it he jumped on me and hugged and kissed me and said, "You see, Mom, Dad *is* home. He *is* home!" He was three years and ten months old, and his premonition had been perfect. We were all relieved that I was safe and healthy, and I was so grateful to be home with my lovely wife and my sweet son.

I started to work for the air force again, travelling at least three hours a day on the bus. I hated the bus trip, so we decided to sell our small apartment and move from Tel Aviv to Holon, a city only thirty minutes from my work. Near the end of 1956, before we moved to Holon, Judit's two sisters, Klara and Éva, arrived from Hungary and moved in with us. They had suffered through the uncertainty of the Hungarian Revolution. Klara, who had been a teacher in Hungary, went to an *ulpan*, a school for new immigrants to learn Hebrew, which was paid for by the government, in Be'er Sheva. Éva lived with us until she got married in August 1958. She had a hard time learning Hebrew because she had decided not to go to an *ulpan*.

In the spring of 1957 I found a duplex in Holon with a good-sized lot where I could plant a garden and grow vegetables and flowers. The land was all sand, like our first house in Netanya, and Paul loved the new house because we had a garden. I planted a guava tree, which grew in its second year and bore three fruit. Paul, though he was a kind-hearted boy, wanted them all for himself. For some reason he felt those three guavas should only be for him. I explained that he had to share with his mother and others, but he still didn't want to listen. I finally convinced him to share and we all agreed they were the best and tastiest guavas we had ever eaten.

Our house was on the border of what we called "no-man's sandy land" because we couldn't see the end of that stretch of land. It went as far as Bat Yam, another city three kilometres from our house that was on the beach. We went there on Saturdays to bathe and play. Paul loved wandering on that empty sandy land with me or Judit. One time he went alone and was lost for a couple of hours, but it was daytime and we found him easily.

Close by was a small Sephardic synagogue and I went there some Friday nights to pray. I found it a little strange the first time I went and heard some of the melodies and songs, which are different, and the Sephardim have different customs as well. For example, the Torah is kept in a wooden cylinder instead of an embroidered cover and it is read in an upright position as opposed to lying flat on a table. The Sephardim also go by other original customs of the Torah – that first Pesach, my neighbour slaughtered a lamb according to Torah custom. It was the first time that I had ever seen that ritual.

During Klara's six-month stay in the Be'er Sheva *ulpan*, she met Mose Jacobs, a Jewish-Canadian teacher originally from Poland who had come to visit the new *ulpan* in Be'er Sheva and, he hoped, to meet a nice Jewish girl to marry. Klara was blond, beautiful and elegant, and the rest is history. When she brought him to our home in Holon to get to know him, we liked him, too. They decided to marry right away because Mose had to go back to his teaching job in Toronto.

The wedding took place in our home in Holon. Altogether there were about twenty-five guests; half were members of Mose's family from Israel and the rest our family. The wedding was simple and warm. Judit made her best fish appetizer. In Hungarian we call it *kocsonya hal*, fish jelly, though most often in gentile homes the *kocsonya*, the jelly, is made from pork. The main entrée was veal, which was hard to get, but Judit had managed to find it at the Yemenite market. We had delicious *tortas,* cakes of all kinds, and Judit made a tasty fruit salad. We sang Hebrew and Yiddish songs. It was a real simcha, a real *chassene*, wedding. Klara and Mose looked lovely together and I gave them my blessing.

~

Although I loved Israel very much, for a variety of reasons, I started to think about leaving. We were now expecting our second child, and Judit and I couldn't earn enough money to buy some things that we wanted, like a car. We both worked for the government, which paid poorly, and sometimes we ran out of money by the end of the month. Also, I had always wanted to be independent, own a business and be my own boss, but in those days it was hard to open a store or do business without a lot of capital. My father still refused to loan or give me money.

Judit and I began to research which country would offer the possibility of an easier life, where we could earn enough money and eventually come back to Israel to open a factory or other business. As we began to ask people questions and read magazines and books about various countries, we found that Brazil had many attractions, one of which was that I had relatives there. Aunt Aranka and Uncle Frici, who had moved to Italy in 1948, had settled in Brazil in 1950, where they owned a knitting factory. It helped to have some family in a new country, so we chose Brazil as our next destination.

Brazil had started to develop its industry after the war and in the 1950s there were many opportunities to manufacture things, such as women's clothing. I wrote to Uncle Frici, explaining that we were coming to Brazil so I could be an independent businessman. I soon learned, however, that we would have to wait at least two years for an Israeli exit visa because I was working in a sensitive military workplace with new technology. In order to start the process, I resigned from my job in the air force in the spring of 1958.

After I left the air force, I looked for something temporary – I didn't want to get a permanent job while we waited for the visa. I wanted to get a taste of the business world and earn more money. I soon found an interesting opportunity with a nice older man who knew of a factory where we could buy comfortable foam rubber mattresses that were a novelty in Israel. He took me on as a partner because he trusted me and needed a young man with good sales skills.

We paid cash for the mattresses and then sold and delivered them to stores. There was a shortage of the mattresses so our business did well and we split the profit fifty-fifty, which was generous of him because he had invested most of the money and used his station wagon to deliver the goods.

On September 10, 1958, our daughter, Iris, was born in Jaffa Hospital. In the early morning I planned to go to the hospital to see Judit and my new baby girl. Paul was almost six and had kindergarten to attend but he insisted on coming with me to see his new sister. So together we met cute baby Iris. She cried day and night until she was five years old, but she was always gorgeous.

The year after Iris was born, we sold our duplex and moved to a rented apartment in Tel Aviv so that we would be ready to go to Brazil. As it turned out, it really wasn't simple to leave Israel. To get an exit visa we needed three things: our income tax had to be paid up to date; I had to provide proof that I had fulfilled my commitment to the army and had been honourably discharged; and we had to get approval from the Sochnut, the Jewish Agency for Israel, proving that we didn't owe the country anything dating back to when we had arrived.

The income tax clearance was easy since I had been employed in Israel for ten years and income tax payments were deducted monthly from my paycheque. The army clearance was a bit more complicated because they checked to make sure I had returned all the army's clothing and equipment when I completed my two-year service, which I had. The third condition ended up being the most surprising – the immigration agency wanted us to pay for a folding bed and mattress they had given Judit at the camp when she had first arrived in Israel. I found it strange, but I had to pay it to get the exit visa. The visa was finally issued after a few weeks; we could leave by August 1960.

Now I had to search for a ship to take us to Brazil. We needed six tickets – one each for me and Judit and the kids, plus another two for a widow named Jojo from Uncle Frici's brother's family, whose husband had died in the Holocaust, and her fifteen-year-old son, Zvika. Uncle Frici wanted both me and Jojo to work in his knitting factory, where he employed more than a hundred workers and needed trustworthy supervisors. My uncle wrote that if I bought the boat tickets from Haifa to Venice for all of us, he would pay for the main part of the trip – from Geneva to Rio de Janeiro. The six tickets cost about three thousand dollars. After having worked for more than ten years in Israel, Judit and I had managed to save about four thousand, which left us with only one thousand for the trip.

We began saying goodbye to friends and family and to pack only the necessities. And after twelve years in Israel – twelve enjoyable but difficult years – our day of departure arrived. I told myself that we were only leaving Israel temporarily. In my mind, I was sure that some day I would come back to the Promised Land for good.

Brazil

In August 1960 we set out from the Port of Haifa to Venice on a small Italian ship. It wasn't a luxury boat, but it was clean, and the food and the service were fine. At our first stop, Cyprus, the ship anchored for a full day. We took the opportunity to go ashore and visit Nicosia and other parts of the island. On the third day, we stopped at the beautiful old port city at Rhodes, an island in Greece. The port didn't have deep water suitable for big ships so the ship anchored about one mile off-shore and we went in by small boats – about twenty people per boat.

Paul was seven and Iris almost two, but she hadn't learned to speak yet. The children were well-behaved and Zvika and Jojo were kind companions. She was a pleasant woman and Judit got along well with her. Judit and I took the kids in a taxi to see the remains of the Temple of Zeus, an ancient altar on top of Attavyros Mountain, an elevation of one thousand metres. The narrow road was only wide enough for one car so it was a dangerous drive, and if I had known, I wouldn't have gone. On our fourth day, we arrived at the southern Italian port city of Bari. We stayed there for a few hours and walked around the port, where we saw a small fruit market selling Israeli oranges – our ship had brought goods from Israel.

The next afternoon, we arrived for a stopover in Venice. The city, with its canals and gorgeous buildings – some of them five hundred years old or more – was wondrous. One thousand years ago, Venice was one of the richest cities in the Mediterranean. We disembarked and went to find a hotel that we could afford near Piazza San Marco, what I thought was the nicest area in the city. I had nine hundred dollars left to pay for the two rooms we needed and food for all of us.

Fortunately, we found a small, clean, affordable hotel for about thirty dollars a night. We got our rooms in the early evening and by the time we had settled in, it had grown dark and we were hungry. Not far from our hotel we found a restaurant with a big fish on a plate in the window. We went inside and sat down, waiting eagerly for our fish dinner. It tasted heavenly – we finished it and everything that came with it. When I asked for the bill, however, and saw it was one hundred dollars, I was shocked. I didn't realize how expensive restaurants were in Venice and had forgotten to ask the price before we ordered. I asked if it was a mistake but the owner said, "No mistake at all." So I paid the bill and, tired from the trip, we went back to the hotel.

The next day we found cheap take-out fried sardines in a nearby market for lunch or dinner, which helped our financial situation. Now I had only just over six hundred dollars to last for the rest of the trip, and we still had to get to Geneva the next day to board the ship that would take us to Brazil. The next morning after breakfast we went to the train station. I bought six tickets to Geneva on the slow train, which cost less but was a five-and-a-half-hour train ride.

On the train, I started a conversation with a nice, older Italian couple. I knew a little Italian because I had studied Portuguese, which has some similarities, during the months before we left Israel. I hated to look for hotels in a city I didn't know so I asked them for the name of a decent, inexpensive hotel in Geneva. They told me about a place that was central, clean, small and affordable.

We arrived at the hotel at 7:00 p.m. The Italian couple had been right, it was inexpensive and clean. Since the boat was not expected to arrive for four days, we had to stay there for three nights. The next day after breakfast we all went for a walk around the city. We went to the Uppin department store, not far from our hotel, to buy luggage, which was much cheaper there than in Israel. We saw a large assortment and bought one piece. When we were ready to leave the store, we couldn't find Iris. She had disappeared. I panicked and we all went out to look for her, running around outside for a half hour before deciding to go back into the store. We were terrified that we had lost her. Thankfully, we found little Iris in the store, holding the saleslady's hand. The saleswoman had heard a voice coming out of a suitcase, opened it and there was Lady Iris, packed away in a suitcase.

Afterward, we went to look for a toy store so that I could buy Paul a toy train, which had been too expensive in Israel. I found a store and Paul chose one big, gorgeous train. It cost almost a hundred dollars – about all the money we had left after the hotel bill had been paid. But fortunately our ship had arrived for the next leg of our journey and the next morning we sailed for Brazil.

Our first stop was Naples, south of Rome, where the ship picked up more travellers and immigrants to Brazil, including a group of thirty or so young priests. The food was mostly Italian and very tasty, and the first two days I had no trouble eating. Once out on the open sea, however, I got seasick and couldn't eat anything for five days. Paul became very friendly with the priests. They wanted to learn Hebrew and when they found out that he was from the Holy Land they played and talked with him all day. My son became their Hebrew teacher and they bought him all kinds of things from the ship's store and gave him chocolate, too. He was really well-behaved; he never complained and was very friendly.

We arrived in Rio de Janeiro on the seventh day. After lunch we had only a little time to walk around the city because the next morning we had to go on to Santos, our final destination. We toured the main street and its beautiful stores all afternoon. But we were shocked and horrified to see so many people sitting, lying down, or actually sleeping on the street with their children and begging for money, food, anything. That sad sight was my introduction to Rio and it made me feel terrible. I was always sensitive to the sufferings of others and this first impression of Brazil made me uncomfortable for months. Like everyone else in Brazil, I slowly got used to it.

The next morning we arrived in Santos, a beautiful port municipality in Brazil, and found my family waiting. We were so happy to see Aunt Aranka and Uncle Frici – their welcome was touching. They were Orthodox and didn't travel on holy days so, because it was just before Shabbat, they took us to a small kosher hotel for a couple of days.

On the third day, we all left Santos for São Paulo – the New York of Brazil. Jojo and Zvika moved into Frici's sister's apartment with her sister-in-law, Iren, her husband, Morris, and their two daughters. They had come from Budapest a few years previously and Morris worked in my uncle's factory. We found a small hotel in a central location and rented a room and kitchen for a couple of months. Although it was furnished, it didn't have a bed suitable for a two-year-old so Iris had to sleep with us until I earned enough money to buy a bed for her – I only had fifty dollars left in my pocket, a decent bed would cost at least two hundred dollars and I still had to buy food. Everything in São Paulo was expensive except for gasoline, which was cheaper than bottled water.

After a day or two I felt ready to work and Uncle Frici gave me the address of a friend who made radios. I went there first thing in the morning. During the interview I told him about my background and expertise in radios and he hired me for a decent hourly wage, which, according to him, was more than he was paying his other employee, a Japanese technician who was more expert than I was. He told me that that particular job was not for a guy like me, which I already knew, but I needed the money to buy my beautiful daughter a bed. So I accepted the job and began working. Unfortunately, he was right – the other man was faster than me. I quit after two weeks, with only enough money to buy food for my family.

The next day I went to my uncle's factory, where Jojo was already working, and told him that I wanted to go to the city to sell his products. I had always loved selling wholesale. He had a salesman for his knitted products but he had large quantities of *renda* fabric, lace, for curtains and bridal gowns. The material was all right but since it was second-rate quality it had accumulated during the last year. He agreed that I could sell it and my commission would be 10 per cent paid promptly in cash. He thought that I would never be able to sell the fabric and I would end up working for him in his factory.

I packed a small suitcase with samples, colours and prices. My uncle told me about a district where wholesale and retail shops carried similar merchandise and might be interested in my wares. I took a streetcar and forty-five minutes later arrived at a large commercial street lined with stores. I saw mannequins with white bridal gowns in many of the windows. Bridal gowns were a thriving business, and women's garments also sold well.

I went into the first store and said, "Bom dia," good day in Portuguese. The owner said that he wasn't interested in looking at the samples. So I said, "Atelogo" – goodbye – and left. The same thing happened in the next store, and the next…. In the sixth store, I went in and said the same "Bom dia" to a tall, elegant man whom I assumed was the owner, and tried to speak to him in Portuguese. He realized that I didn't really speak Portuguese and asked if we could talk in English. He looked at my samples for a few minutes and asked how many metres we had of the material he liked. I told him that we had a lot – maybe 10,000 metres or more. He asked me to wait a few minutes, then said he wanted to go to the factory with me to see the goods. So we got in his car, which was a Jaguar. Cars were expensive in Brazil, so I knew that he must have been quite well off. We arrived at the factory in twenty minutes and, luckily, my uncle was there. I introduced him to the storekeeper and they went into the warehouse while I stayed in the office so as not to interfere with the negotiations.

After an hour they came back to the office and my uncle told me that the man had bought the entire stock and paid 10,000 dollars cash. Then, I knew that I would be able to afford to buy the bed for Iris. I was paid one thousand dollars and was so excited to have earned my first big commission that I went straight home and told the whole story to Judit. That same evening we went to buy Iris's bed and I bought the best one in the store.

I now had enough money for two months' rent and we could afford to lease a one-bedroom apartment. We found a modern apartment in a good middle-class neighbourhood on Alameda Barao de Limeira Street. It was close to the main street and Aunt Aranka's apartment, which we visited frequently. Three weeks later, we moved in. In 1960, rent was fairly high in Brazil, but buying a condo, which were just starting to be built, was fairly cheap by comparison. Judit and I made a big mistake in not buying a condo right away, since prices got higher every year. Returning to Israel with financial stability was always in the back of our minds and this thinking ended up costing us a lot of money: the dollar lost value every year but properties appreciated quite a bit.

After my good fortune on the first fabric sale, I took more samples from my uncle's factory and went out selling again. First, I went to the garment district of Bom Retiro – the centre of Brazil's wholesale and manufacturing garment business. Buyers came from as far as 2,500 kilometres away to buy fashionable clothing for women and men. Most of the stores had Jewish owners, though a few were of Greek origin. I sold knitwear from my uncle's factory and materials to women's clothing manufacturers.

One day I went into a small establishment with a sign outside that said Manufacturers of Ladies Sportswear. It turned out to be a three-room factory. After I told the owner my name, he said, "I am Mr. Szanto and my wife and I speak Hungarian." He had been a tailor in Budapest and had come to Brazil in 1956 during the Hungarian Revolution; they were now in their mid- to late fifties. Mr. Szanto cut the fabrics and his wife, as well as other women who worked from home, sewed them. These women took home enough material for thirty or more skirts and brought back the finished product – well-made women's pleated and straight skirts – two days later. I spoke with Mr. Szanto for a long time and after I left, I called on him a few times. On the third occasion, he asked if I could sell his products, too, as he didn't have the time.

I started selling his wares as well as delivering them and collecting the money. The skirts were popular and stores wanted more. I earned only commission on these skirts, but did quite well. After a few months, Mr. Szanto and I became good friends. He had developed complete trust in me and asked me to be his equal partner. I had some money saved but didn't need to invest much. What he needed was me and good fabric to make the skirts.

So, after almost one year in Brazil, for the first time in my life, I had my own business. I was proud of my accomplishment because no one had given me any financial help.

Judit had found a job as the director of one of the religious schools in São Paulo. The school was a little far and she had to wake up early and go by bus but she never complained. She loved her job and everybody loved her at the school, including the children's parents. She was very dedicated.

I woke up at 6:00 a.m. or earlier every weekday to take Iris and Paul to their Jewish schools, which started at 7:00 a.m. and went until 1:00 p.m. The schools were in Bom Retiro, about a fifteen-minute drive from our home. The children liked their schools and after one year they spoke Portuguese fluently. Judit and I also learned Portuguese, a much easier language to learn than English.

At 7:00 a.m. I started visiting my customers. Most of the wholesale stores opened at 7:00 or 7:30 a.m. and closed for siesta between 1:00 and 4:00 p.m. so the staff could go home for lunch and rest. I did the same.

One of my clients, Sandor Kovari, whose nickname was Sanyi, rented a two-storey building on a main street. The ground floor was quite large and the second floor, which was the same size, was empty except for a long cutting table. After a few months, Sanyi and I got to be friends. He was a perfect gentleman – calm and patient with everyone. He organized his stock well, but he wasn't a great businessman. His wife, Renée, had a better sense of business. Their son, Andris, was soon a good friend of Paul's – they were the same age but went to different schools.

In 1962, my father and Magda immigrated to Brazil and rented an apartment close to Aunt Aranka. My father had been active his whole life and had to work, so he got a job in my uncle's factory as a warehouse supervisor, checking outgoing orders and keeping everything running smoothly. After awhile, he started to lend people money to earn interest and grew obsessed with risking his money to make a profit. He had lost half of his money that way in Israel and he started making the same mistake in São Paulo. He loaned money to a Hungarian man who had a quality glove factory, but during the recession in 1967, the man's business went down the drain. My father lost thousands of dollars. My father never wanted to tell me about his money-lending activities because he knew I was against it. I only became aware of his involvement with the glove business when the owner got into financial trouble and my father asked me to try to get all or part of his money back.

I was busy with my business and soon had enough to buy a used car, an old, red Chrysler DeSoto. Almost two years into my partnership with Szanto I entered a new partnership with Sandor Kovari. I had money to go in with him but we didn't need much because I could make cash sales. Buyers came from all over Brazil to buy our pleated skirts.

I had learned how to be a cutter from Szanto and I cut the material with the help of our employee, Maria. We were busy and I was working eleven hours a day, with an hour off for lunch. Maria and I got along well with Sanyi, who went along with my ideas most of the time. I enjoyed much more profit with him than I had in the previous business because we manufactured and sold our products ourselves.

In June 1967, when I was thirty-six, war broke out between Israel and Egypt, Jordan and Syria and the consulate in São Paulo told us that Israel might need volunteers. I went to the consulate to register to go if they needed me. Fortunately, the Israeli Air Force wiped out the Egyptian air force completely in the first air attack and in just six days Israel had won the war, which came to be known as the Six-Day War. Israel didn't end up needing volunteers, but I was ready and willing to defend Israel – which all Jewish people have to do.

~

At the beginning of 1968, we were looking forward to living in a bigger apartment that we had bought in 1966 at an early construction discount from a Jewish builder. It was to be quite a luxurious and modern three-bedroom apartment on an elegant street. We had had to make a down payment plus additional instalments every three months, and the apartment was supposed to be ready in two years. We were pleased with our purchase, but the construction went slowly. Although everybody paid quarterly, two years later the building was only half finished.

One evening, the builder called a meeting of all the buyers – about eighty families or more – to explain the delay and ask for extra money. I strongly suspected that the delay was deliberate – there were no strikes in the industry. He just wanted more money. So I stood up and started to speak against him and the delays. Everybody applauded. We were all mostly young couples and needed the apartments. I was paying five hundred dollars rent every month, which at that time was a lot of money.

After the meeting, the builder called me into his office and asked me not to instigate a revolt. He wanted to know what it would take for me agree to his proposal for a delay. I told him that I wanted my apartment ready in three month's time, not another year or year and a half. He promised me that we could move in, at the latest, in three months.

Three months later, in the spring of 1968, just as the recession was starting to worsen, we moved in all right, but the building wasn't ready – the elevators weren't working, the hallways weren't finished and only our apartment was habitable. We lived alone in the building for about six months and it was only completely finished after another ten months. But I saved some money by moving in early and we finally had our home.

We lived well in São Paulo. We had a live-in maid who also knew how to cook, and Judit loved the fact that she had the best and most famous couturier in town to make her suits. On weekends we often went to the famous beaches of Guarujá and the beautiful beaches of Santos, which was developing into a resort city. We went to the wide and white sandy beaches every Saturday and Sunday. It was heaven for the kids. We also went to Praia Azul where there was a Hungarian resort with amazing food and a beach.

That spring, my partner Sanyi told me that he had a heart condition and he and his family were preparing to return to Budapest, where his brother lived and where he wanted to receive his medical treatment. He left Brazil and, for the first time, I was left alone with the business.

In the winter of 1968, when Paul had a vacation from school, he came to the store and told me that he wanted to try to sell my garments in stores. He was only fourteen and a half, but he asked me to give him samples, prices and an order book. I was surprised, but his effort made me proud. I asked him where he wanted to sell and he said that he would try the coastal tourist cities of Santos and Guarujá. I wished my son good luck and off he went. At that time we were deep into a recession and sales were tough. I said to myself, at least he is trying and willing to earn money. Paul actually came back from the trip with a lot of orders. I sent the materials and paid Paul 10 per cent as well as his trip expenses. He continued to work a few more times during his vacation from school. However, as Brazil's depression worsened, my business started to lose money for the first time, which was quite a shock. Fortunately, Judit had a good salary and we managed not to dip into our savings.

We liked the people of São Paulo and had a good life there but an ill-wind was starting to blow, bringing hard times and riots and huge unemployment. One day thousands rioted in a Rio de Janeiro suburb, breaking store windows and shouting, "Get out all strangers," which of course included Jews. We had heard Jews called "strangers" there before. With the unemployment sharply rising, crime was greatly increasing.

On another day, Judit walked to the grocery store to buy milk and a man stole her purse. Thank God she wasn't hurt. She shouted for someone to catch the thief but another woman warned her to be quiet or the thief might come back and kill her. I didn't feel safe there anymore and we began to think long and hard about whether to leave Brazil. I worried about our children's future, about what kind of future they could have in a country where most of the people only earned about fifty dollars a month – if they could find work. That wasn't even enough to pay rent for one room. I also started having bad dreams, probably from both the Holocaust and the social and political situation in Brazil. I couldn't bear the thought of my children being persecuted. Maybe I was being too protective, but when we told the kids we were thinking about leaving, we were surprised that Iris and Paul didn't resist at all. They behaved like grown-ups although Iris was only eleven and Paul sixteen. Still, the decision to leave Brazil was difficult. Our children had adjusted to their schools, had close friends, and their grandfather lived nearby. Iris had been going to a ballet class for a few years and was developing into a beautiful girl. For a few months, Paul had gone to the best yeshiva high school in Petrópolis, a beautiful elite mountain city close to Rio de Janeiro.

After some discussion, Judit and I decided that the best place to go was Toronto, where Judit's sister Klara lived, as did Uncle Sándor, who had moved there in 1951 with his wife, Olga. Aunt Lili and Uncle Jenő had also lived in Toronto since 1956 though, sadly, Uncle Jenő died of a heart attack in 1963 at the relatively young age of sixty-four. He had had a heart condition for many years and at that time there weren't many drugs available and it wasn't easy to get heart bypass surgery. Uncle Jenő was a calm, patient person whom I had always had great conversations with. He reminded me of my paternal grandfather.

What finally sold us on Toronto was thinking back to our trip to North America in the spring of 1964. Judit and I had taken an airplane for the first time and went to the World's Fair in New York City. We rented a room in Brooklyn, where we had friends and relatives, including Iren and Morris and their two daughters, who had moved there from Brazil. New York made a good impression on us, especially Fifth Avenue, Broadway and all the interesting buildings.

After ten days in New York we had taken a bus to Toronto and stayed for a week at Klara's house. We toured Toronto to get to know it better. My brother-in-law Mose took us almost everywhere and one day the four of us and the children went to the Yorkdale Mall, which was then only a few months old and the only big mall in the city. When Mose parked the car in the parking lot he left the windows and the doors open and his purchases in the car. I asked him why he didn't lock the car – wouldn't somebody steal his things? He and Klara told us that in Toronto nobody would steal anything and that they left the house unlocked, too. Judit and I liked that a lot.

Toronto made an excellent impression on us. It was spotless and we didn't see any *favelas* or shanties without running water or sewers like the slums that were everywhere in Rio and São Paulo. I had a positive feeling after the visit to Toronto, a sense that it would offer my children a better future, so when things began to deteriorate in Brazil, our thoughts returned to Canada and Toronto.

From the time I submitted our application to the Canadian embassy in São Paulo we had to wait at least a year to get our visa to enter Canada. In order to be able to immigrate, we had to have a few medical tests and I had to get a work contract from a company in Toronto. I found an electrical contracting firm that was willing to hire me as an electrician but I couldn't begin liquidating my business while we were waiting for permanent visas from the Canadian embassy. The next ten months or so were nerve-wracking. Tons of businesses went broke in São Paulo; factories closed; Jews and Greeks left the country in droves.

Finally, in the summer of 1969, we received a letter from the Canadian embassy that we had been granted visas to enter Canada that would expire on May 6, 1970. The letter from the Canadian embassy stated that we had to make an appointment to come in person to the embassy to receive the visas from the ambassador. When Judit and I went to see the ambassador, he received us warmly and asked us when we wanted to leave for Canada. The school year in Brazil finished in December so we thought we would leave for Toronto at the end of the year. The ambassador strongly advised us not to arrive in Canada before the end of April due to the harsh Canadian winter. He thought we might get fed up with the weather. We sat with him for about thirty minutes, then he put the visas in our hands and I thanked him for his advice. The ambassador was wise to warn us about winter in Toronto.

At that point I had about four months to sell our apartment, most of our things and liquidate the business. We got lucky with selling the apartment – we got double the price we had paid and the buyer also bought many of the furnishings. I sold my old Chrysler DeSoto for the same price that I had paid for it six years before.

After we got our visas, Judit and I went to a travel agency to buy airplane tickets to Los Angeles. We had decided to take the ambassador's advice about not arriving in Toronto until the end of April, and made plans to spend four months in Los Angeles, where our friend Eli Niv, whom we had met in Brazil, lived. I was sure that the kids would like it there, especially Paul. He was interested in producing films and Hollywood was the place to learn about it.

When we went to the travel agency, we were told we could pay fifty dollars more per ticket and fly over the whole continent of South

America. We agreed right away to such an unexpected adventure for such a reasonable price. I bought the four tickets and the countdown to our departure, December 26, 1969, began.

We were all excited about the trip. Judit, Iris and I had Brazilian passports; Paul was not yet eligible for a Brazilian passport, so he still had an Israeli passport. We said goodbye to my father, Magda, Aunt Aranka, Uncle Frici and my cousins Tomàs and Vera. I didn't think that I would ever see my older relatives again. Unfortunately, I had never had the best relationship with my father and Magda.

On December 24, 1969, two days before we left Brazil, we decided to spend an evening downtown with the kids to enjoy São Paulo's night life for the last time and to say goodbye. We had dinner in a lovely restaurant and then walked around. Since it was just before Christmas, all the stores were open late. I wanted to buy a souvenir for Judit, but I didn't know what. Suddenly, in the window of a jewellery store, we saw a beautiful ring with a brilliant blue stone, like the bluest sky on a perfect day. I looked at Judit and asked her if she wanted it. She loved it. It was a forty-karat gemstone and we all went into the store to ask the price. The saleslady told us that it was a genuine stone and we would get a certificate of guarantee from the largest jewellery firm in Brazil, H. Stern. And then she told me the wholesale price – two thousand dollars. I saw the look on Judit's face. She loved both the stone and the ring, and I loved Judit, so I bought her that perfect stone, a special memento of Brazil.

Journey to North America

After our wonderful farewell evening in São Paulo, we were all ready for our next destination. The first country we visited was Uruguay, about a three-hour flight south from São Paulo. Montevideo, the capital of Uruguay, was a small city of about a million people and it was clean, quiet and charming. We stayed there for two nights, exploring both the city's beauty and the steak restaurants, which were some of the best in the world. We tasted lamb steaks for the first time, cut from a whole small lamb that had been slowly roasted over a huge barbecue. We enjoyed those two days enormously.

On December 29 we flew to Buenos Aires, the capital of Argentina. The city was huge compared to Montevideo and with its elegance, massive monuments and government buildings, very different from São Paulo or Rio De Janeiro. The main avenue in central Buenos Aires is 9 de Julio, the widest avenue in the world.

Argentina exports a lot of leather, so Buenos Aires was full of leather stores. We went to the best restaurants and bought leather goods. I didn't need to save money anymore the way I had on the trip to Brazil. Now, I had plenty to spend. We liked the city but it was their summer and extremely hot. We asked at the hotel where we could go to bathe or swim and they suggested a beach in Río de la Plata, not far from the city. We went there the next day and were astonished to see that the delta of the river was so wide that it looked like the ocean.

The water was a strange kind of salt water mixed with sweet water, but it was clean and calm so we could swim. We stayed there almost the whole day.

The next day was New Year's Eve and Judit and I decided that we would celebrate as we always did, by touring night clubs all night. Paul stayed with Iris at the hotel and they watched TV all night. One of the clubs we went to had Argentine folkloric dances with Argentine-Spanish tangos and step dances. The whole night was fabulous – a real celebration of bringing in the New Year 1970.

The next day we rested before our trip to Peru. We had wanted to go to Mexico City, but couldn't get a visa right away for Paul because of his Israeli passport; I think because it was from a different continent. The Mexican embassy in Buenos Aires told us that we would have to wait at least two months to get a visa. The rest of us, who had Brazilian passports, could get visas within a half hour, which was frustrating.

On January 2, 1970, we took a plane across the Andes Mountains, the tallest mountain range in South America. The plane flew just above the peaks and sometimes I felt that we might touch one of them accidentally. I can still see the beauty and height of those peaks. We flew through those enormous mountains for about an hour. It was spectacular but scary. There were no clouds and we enjoyed the perfect visibility.

We arrived in Lima late in the morning and promptly took a taxi to the city. All the taxi drivers were natives, which scared us a little because they looked so foreign to us. When we arrived in the city centre, we started exploring the area on foot. The main street was wide and long, but the city was no match for Buenos Aires or Montevideo. Lima is a poor but clean city. It's on a high altitude and the air is fresh. As we walked along the main street we saw windows full of silver – huge silver plates of all kinds, silver figures, silver animals, birds, cups, everything made of silver – and all were sparkling in the sunshine. At that time, Lima was the centre of silver goods for

South America as well as the US. We had a late lunch in a restaurant in the city square and afterward took in the beautiful architecture of the buildings, especially the Government Palace.

At 5:30 p.m. we had to go back to the airport for our 9:00 p.m. flight to Los Angeles. We didn't want to take a taxi because we still didn't feel comfortable with the drivers, so we waited for a bus – a trip of about twenty minutes. As we were waiting, a private car stopped and a well-dressed gentleman got out and asked us in Spanish where we wanted to go. When we told him, he offered to take us there. He told us that he worked in the air traffic control tower and soon struck up a conversation with Paul, who is a real people person. They talked about the tower and when we arrived our driver offered to take Paul up to the tower and show him the whole air-traffic-control operation. Paul was thrilled.

We landed in Los Angeles at 5:00 a.m. and after we went through customs, we were surprised and delighted to find our good friend Eli Niv, who was waiting to drive us to his home. When we arrived at his ranch-style bungalow in Hollywood, his wife, Yael, received us with open arms and a lovely welcome. After a few minutes they showed us our bedroom, which to our surprise was their bedroom – a big suite with a bathroom. The kids got separate bedrooms too. We were very moved. I didn't want to accept their offer of separate bedrooms, but they insisted.

We stayed with them for five days until I found a nice four-plex not far from their house – all furnished with three bedrooms on one level and a big courtyard. The owner asked for two hundred dollars a month but told me if I would put out the garbage three times a week and take care of the garden I could have the apartment for 160 dollars a month. I promptly agreed. I loved to do gardening and was happy to save a bit. Our new home was on Martel Avenue close to Santa Monica Boulevard. We weren't far from film producer Samuel Goldwyn's first studio which, although old, was still open. One block from our home was a food and department store called Boys' Market that later became a source of entertainment for us, especially for Paul and Iris. We went there every day except weekends to buy chickens and chicken parts for barbecuing. "The best barbecued chickens in the world" according to Paul and Iris – maybe because they chose the chickens and barbecued them themselves. The Boys' Market had so many products that were unknown in Brazil. Everything was new and different in Los Angeles.

On the Monday morning after that first weekend, I took Iris to the closest public school. I had heard from our friends that that particular school welcomed visiting children and allowed them to attend regular classes. I was ready to pay for the school because I didn't want Paul and Iris to lose a few months of their studies, and also I wanted them to learn English since it was one of the official languages spoken in Canada.

Iris and I arrived half an hour before classes started. The principal welcomed us and asked for some basic information and then, to my surprise, she said, "Now I will take her to her new class." I asked how much the school would cost a month and she replied, "Nothing." I was amazed and I said to myself, That is the United States of America.

After that, Paul and I went to the nearby Fairfax High School, which I had been told was the best in the city. It was the same situation, the same welcome, and he too began school immediately. I went home alone and told the whole story to Judit. She was surprised, too. Paul loved Fairfax High – the school was excellent and had high standards. Iris also loved her school and after just a few weeks she began to speak English pretty well.

Our friends Eli and Yael wanted us to have friends in the city and introduced us to one of Yael's girlfriends whose parents were Hungarian. She was a gracious and friendly woman named Lidia who knew many people in LA. Through her, we met Tibor Adler and his wife, Vera, who had a daughter the same age as Paul. Tibor was a builder and Vera worked as a secretary in an insurance company. They lived in a ranch bungalow in Beverly Hills.

The Adlers invited us, along with Eli and Yael, to a dinner to get to know us better. We expected a small dinner party, so when we arrived and found thirty people there, we were amazed. The dinner was a surprise party in honour of our arrival and all of their friends and friends' friends were invited – many of them Hungarian. There were teachers, engineers of all kinds and manufacturers. One of the engineers, Hegyesi, had been at the Xerox company since its beginning. He was an intelligent man married to a Hungarian gentile. They were a down-to-earth couple, always ready to go on road trips and we went touring with them many times. The welcome was extremely lovely and the evening excellent. We talked about our experiences in Brazil and everyone listened intently. We made new friends and later received many invitations to parties from them.

I also became good friends with Jancsi Rado, who lived with his wife in a nice house with a swimming pool on a small hill overlooking the Los Angeles Valley and Hollywood. Jancsi had a manufacturing shop where he made one kind of airplane screw for the Boeing Company. He was pleasant and his dream, because he loved beautiful clothing, was to own an elegant men's shop in Beverly Hills. I don't think he ever accomplished his dream but he worked until he was seventy-six and then retired.

Our new friend Tibor Adler was an exceptional man and right after the party he invited us to stay in the US. He said that he was willing to arrange work for Judit in the Hebrew School in Beverly Hills – he had already made an appointment for her with the head of the school the next morning at 10:00 a.m. and would pick us up at 9:30. We hesitated at first, but Judit and I agreed that we should go for an interview.

The principal of the school told Judit that they needed Hebrew teachers and that he would hire her, but we needed to apply for a green card. He gave her a letter stating that the school was willing to hire her. After that we had to decide if we wanted to stay in the United States, since we now had a letter of intent from the school. We decided to go to an immigration lawyer Tibor recommended. The lawyer, a nice Jewish guy, explained that the procedure could take six to eight months and asked for half the fee he usually charged. I figured it was worth a try since the kids and Judit loved LA. I, however, wasn't thrilled with the city. It felt like a huge village and since I am sensitive to temperature changes, I wasn't comfortable with the fluctuations in temperature: cool in the morning and late afternoon and very hot at midday.

The lawyer started the process and after we had been in LA for about two months he called and asked us to come to his office to discuss the matter. When we got there, he told us that it would be possible for us to get green cards and stay in the US legally, but Paul, who was almost eighteen, would be required to register for the draft and fight in the Vietnam War. I replied that my son would only belong to one army and that was the Israel Defense Forces. Vietnam was out of the question. The lawyer was extremely gracious, wished us good luck and even gave me back my money.

Now we knew that we would have to leave the United States. We made plans to drive to Toronto in our comfortable, air-conditioned light-beige Chevrolet Impala and arrive at the beginning of May. The speedometer had 130,000 miles on it – we had logged approximately seven thousand miles on the car touring Los Angeles, the suburbs and the surrounding small communities – and it had not needed an oil change. The previous owner had been a playboy and had had it for a few years. I worried about it breaking down on the highway, but realized that I could always buy a new car along the way if the Impala failed.

Until our departure, we kept busy. We went to the original Disneyland a few times, which was excellent fun. We also went to the beach at Malibu, about a fifteen-minute drive from our home. It was a wide sandy beach with lots of young people playing ball or lying in the sun. Hardly anyone went in the water, which I found curious, so I decided to test the waters. After only about two seconds, however,

I ran straight out. It was freezing. Not only was the ocean frigid in April, it was cold all year round.

Paul and I worked part-time in a drive-through milk distribution store about twenty minutes from our house in Hollywood. The job paid well. The owner was a Hungarian-Jewish man in his late fifties I had met by chance and, when we got to know each other he offered me the job because he trusted me. All the milk sales were in cash and lots of milk was sold every day.

~

We left Los Angeles for Toronto on the morning of April 30, 1970. We loaded our car with the many purchases we had made in California and started out on the famous Route 66, the first highway that connected the United States from west to east. Judit was excellent at reading maps, so she navigated. Since the North 66 was closed in the spring because of the weather, we took the southern route toward Las Vegas. On the way we drove through a sandstorm, which was a common occurrence in Nevada. When we arrived in Las Vegas at noon and checked into a motel-hotel with a small swimming pool on the Strip, the main street in Las Vegas, I noticed the sandstorm had stripped the paint off the front of the car.

It was a bit chilly in Las Vegas but there was lots of sunshine so we ate lunch and went to explore the city, which at that time was mainly the Strip. The buildings were low-rise motel types and there were lots of casinos, most of them much smaller than today. I played a little without any luck, but didn't lose too much money. I was always careful.

The next morning, we headed to one of the biggest power plants in the United States, the Hoover Dam, about fifty kilometres from Vegas. It is a huge engineering marvel of the twentieth century and the Colorado River is extremely fast. We arrived there before noon and took a guided tour inside the dam. The elevator took four minutes to go all the way down to the bottom. We were all surprised at the grandeur of the Hoover Dam.

After lunch we travelled toward Arizona and Grand Canyon National Park. We stopped there for a few hours to take in the beauty of the canyon and the breathtaking view. Then we drove on to Santa Fe, New Mexico, stopped briefly in Kansas and then went on to St. Louis, Missouri, where we stayed on the outskirts of town. On the fifth day, we came to the end of Route 66 in Chicago. Judit navigated the entire trip and read the maps extraordinarily well so we never got lost. I had the most beautiful and talented tour guide in the world.

On the sixth day, we arrived at the US/Canada border at Detroit/Windsor. I went into the customs office, where there were few custom agents on duty, with my papers that elapsed on May 7, the very next day. We had to wait an hour for the agent to clear the car, which he could not do until the head of the department returned from lunch at about 1:00 p.m. A friendly Jewish man, he explained the procedure for importing the car and gave us clearance to pass through the border.

We took the 401 highway from Windsor and arrived in Toronto at about 5:30 p.m. We were looking for Bathurst Street and Sheppard Avenue where Klara lived, but we couldn't find the exit for Bathurst. There was no sign of it at all. We kept going, passing the widest part of the 401 through Scarborough, until I realized that we were heading out of Toronto. So we turned around and after driving back west we finally found Bathurst Street. Later, we realized that there wasn't an exit for Bathurst on the eastbound 401. We found Klara's house and everyone was happy to see us.

My intention was to buy a house right away so that we didn't stay too long at Klara's. The very next day I began looking in the area near Alexis Boulevard and Bathurst, south of Sheppard, and found a bungalow for sale. The following day Judit and I went to see it, but the price was 32,000 dollars – a lot at that time – and Judit didn't like it. So we decided that it was too early to buy a house and that we would lease an apartment instead. We found a nice two-bedroom apartment with an outdoor swimming pool north of Finch Avenue on Cedarcroft Boulevard. It was a new building, the rent was two hundred dollars a month and for signing a two-year lease I got two months rent-free. We moved in after a week or so.

Paul started attending William Lyon Mackenzie Collegiate, which had a large Jewish student population and a lot of middle-class boys. He liked it very much. Iris went to R. J. Lang Junior High School and had a good teacher and guide, Mr. McCaul. The school was close to our new home. She made a few girlfriends, including one of her best friends named Angie.

During the first year in Toronto we adjusted to our new lives and tried to make as many friends as we could. In late June, we met a young couple, Danny and Katy Ebrani, and their three sons at our building's swimming pool. They lived in the building north of us and came to our pool to swim. Danny was born in Iran and Katy was born in Hungary. They had lived and married in Israel and had arrived in Canada a year before us.

Judit took a six-month course in English for newcomers at George Brown College, where she met Brazilian-born Helga Valentine, whose Jewish husband, Gimi, worked in an export-import company. They had two nice boys who became friends with Paul and Iris.

I started to work as a salesman again, selling Italian sweaters and pullovers. The boss, Steven Douglas, was a friend and distant family member of Uncle Sándor, and the firm was called Steven Douglas & Company. It was located on Adelaide Street at Spadina Avenue and my sales territory was Toronto and Northern Ontario. I got two suitcases of samples, a big one for men's wear and a smaller one for women's pullovers. There were two other sales reps – one for the rest of Ontario and one for Western Canada and British Columbia.

The salesperson for Ontario was an elegant Jewish playboy about ten years older than me whose father had owned a ladies' coat factory. When we got to know each other, he told me that my enthusiasm was appreciated but that I had to be realistic. For any salesman only one thing was certain – expenses. You could always count on having costs, he said, but you couldn't count on sales. He was right, of course, but that didn't deter me. I had a strong will and a family to support.

Judit finished the English course but didn't want to go back into teaching. She was good at fitting and altering garments and wanted to learn the retail fashion business, so she got a job doing alterations in an established ladies' wear store owned by an elderly Jewish woman. The shop was on Yonge Street, north of the North York City Hall and not too far from our apartment. Although business was good and there were lots of alterations, Judit was not paid well. Nonetheless, she achieved her goal of learning the ladies' wear boutique business and got the Canadian experience she needed. She worked there about eight months.

Meanwhile, I had been searching for and finally found a suitable store for Judit to own. It was not very big, but had been established for thirty years and was in a good location – Yonge and Eglinton, across the street from the current Sporting Life store. The name of the store was The Jane Frock Shoppe and the owner, also an elderly woman, wanted to sell. We bought the store along with some of the merchandise.

After being in Toronto for only fifteen months, Judit now had her own profitable boutique. Her clients were mostly older Canadian women who liked to dress elegantly and wanted their clothes to fit perfectly, so Judit had a lot of alterations to do.

My work involved a lot of driving around, making sales and trying to establish regular clients. I was paid 10 per cent of every sale delivered and once a month for delivered garments. I was responsible for all my expenses, but gas was cheap and lunches inexpensive. Every day for lunch I ate soup and a hamburger, which cost about one dollar. I made a lot of client connections and made friends with some of them, too. I earned enough money to cover all our home expenses and we saved the profit from Judit's store.

Iris loved her new high school, Newtonbrook Secondary School, and that's where she met her future husband, Darrel Yashinsky, a blond Jewish boy who was born in Toronto. They hardly knew each other then, but Darrel later admitted that he always noticed Iris – he had wanted to get to know her, but he was shy. With his blond hair, Iris was pretty sure that he was a goyish boy and she knew that we wouldn't want her to date someone who wasn't Jewish. Judit and I had talked a lot about that with Iris and Paul.

By the time we arrived in Toronto, Aunt Lili had been a widow for seven years. She was lonely and happy that we had come. Her only son, Iván, lived in the US and rarely visited. For the next thirteen years, until she passed away, we visited her almost every week and spent a lot of time together. She came to our home frequently and she loved to sit on our big couch in the living room, where it was sunny. She had never wanted to marry again, independent until her last day.

After two years of working hard and enduring two harsh winters in Toronto, we decided to go to Florida for two weeks, to a hotel named Twelve Caesars at Bal Harbour on the ocean near Miami. After that, for many years, we vacationed on different Caribbean islands. We had always wanted to go back to Brazil, but instead visited Israel or Hungary, where my sister and her family lived. Brazil was a good memory for all of us, but now seemed too far and remote.

Two years after we moved into the apartment at Cedarcroft and Bathurst, we found a three-bedroom apartment in a fairly new building on Ridelle Avenue near Marlee Avenue. It was one of the first high-rise buildings to have a pool on the top floor. The view from the pool was spectacular, especially at night. I signed a two-year lease at $260 a month and we all loved the place.

Before we moved to our new place I got a phone call from Aunt Aranka that my father had died. He had been in the hospital and after two days had had a fatal stroke. I sat shiva and we had a minyan every evening. Every day after that, I went to say Kaddish. The funeral was already over by the time I got the news so I didn't see a reason to go to Brazil.

I had gotten a long letter from my father a few months before he died, complaining about money issues with Aunt Aranka and the whole Friedlander family. There had been a family dispute over finances and they never wrote back when I sent them a letter about it. The last time I heard from that side of the family was after Aunt Aranka died. I got a letter from Uncle Frici, saying that he was sick and alone and that he should have died first, not Aranka. I was touched that he wrote me, but I wondered, why me? He died a few months later at age eighty-five.

In the summer of 1974, we decided that it was time to buy a house and began seriously looking. When we drove along Steeles Avenue, east of Bathurst, we saw a sign that said "Renovated Rental Townhouses Now For Sale." We went in to look at the finished ones and made the deal right away, choosing a corner unit on the inner row, not facing Steeles Avenue, that had more lawn space. The complex also had underground and aboveground parking. In our townhouse we had a finished basement, a kitchen, a sliding door to a patio and an open garden. Judit decorated with mirrors and wallpaper and it looked beautiful. We felt at home and were surrounded by a close community of friendly neighbours, many of whom were Israeli.

In our second year there, we had a New Year's party. There were twenty-eight people packed into the small basement, but it was a lovely party and our friends never forgot that evening. As the Hungarian saying goes: "Good people can be accommodated in a small place, too."

Meanwhile, Paul finished high school and went to York University to get his bachelor of science degree. He still hadn't decided what profession to pursue. I suggested that he study law because he was a good student and was great in public relations but he told me he didn't know English well enough to be a lawyer. He went to a chiropractic college instead, but I knew that didn't suit his nature and that he wouldn't be happy there. I didn't discourage him, though; I let him make his own mistakes. He quit after a year and a half and eventually went on to become a car dealer. Paul had always loved cars and enjoyed his work.

By the time Iris had grown up and graduated from high school, in 1977, we had been living in the townhouse for two and a half years and now wanted more bedrooms and a garden of our own. I always loved gardening, planting flowers, bushes and trees, but we couldn't do that in the townhouse complex because all the garden maintenance could only be done by the management. At the same time, we had a new store at St. Clair Avenue and Yonge Street – a great location. I was responsible for buying stock and Judit was an excellent saleslady – one of the best – and had lots of regular customers.

We got an offer for our townhouse and started to look for a house that sat on its own lot, a home where Judit and I could plant flowers as we wished. We had heard that the Bayview Avenue area was a nice neighbourhood, so we told our real estate agent that we wanted to live around Bayview and Finch. After showing us different houses, she said that she had a perfect home for us and took us to 46 Colonnade Road. But it was winter, the end of February, with a lot of snow on the ground, so although we liked the house, we could only see that the pool was covered with snow. The owners took out their pictures of the kidney-shaped pool in summer. Both Judit and I love to swim, so, after a little bargaining, we bought the house.

The house was in perfect condition except for the wallpaper in the entrance hall, which we eventually changed. The owner left us a huge, long freezer and the day after we moved in Judit wanted to sell it or throw it away. But I saved the freezer and after a few months, Judit fell in love with its practicality. The previous owners also sold us a table-tennis set that was in the basement, which later became the most popular sport for all of us, including our grandchildren. Our grandchildren's second-favourite sport always was and still is wrestling. They love to get together and roughhouse, including Dalia, my granddaughter.

We weren't able to use the pool much when we moved in because the weather hadn't been great that summer, but in August we decided that we would have a pool party for about thirty of our friends. We prayed for warm weather. Our prayers were answered and that last August weekend was the best and warmest of the summer. The party was great. Some of our Brazilian friends were younger and liked to drink beer and lots of vodka and I, of course, had to drink with them. After a few hours, many of us, including a few of the women, were quite drunk. It never occurred to me to do anything extraordinary or unusual but then one guy took off his swimming suit and jumped into the pool naked. A few seconds later I followed, as did many of our friends. Not Judit, though; she was always shy. So our party turned into a skinny-dipping-pool-party, and we all talked about it for a long time after.

Paul only brought a girlfriend home on rare occasions. One, Genis, was a window decorator who was likeable, intelligent and business-oriented, but not Jewish. When Paul invited her to our home for a day we knew that they might be getting more serious. After a long conversation with her I learned that she was willing to convert to Judaism if Paul would marry her. I was ready to accept her as a daughter-in-law, but we hadn't met her large family. In mixed marriages the person who converts has learned our traditions ahead of time and accepts our laws; he or she has chosen to be Jewish. But I think it is different for their families, who have different holidays and religious laws and may not accept our way of life. Even marriages within Judaism, between Orthodox and non-Orthodox Jews, have problems that often lead to divorce. I know of many examples of mixed marriages in which these difficulties have arisen.

In the end, Paul's relationship with Genis only lasted a few months. I think that Paul wasn't ready to get married. Like my father, he wanted to remain a bachelor as long as he could. If not for my grandmother Bertha's strong intervention – she told my father she would cut him off if he didn't marry – he would never have married. He married quite late, as did Paul.

When Iris turned twenty, in the summer of 1978, she wanted to take a two- or three-month trip to Israel, the land of her birth. Since we had emigrated from Israel when she was only one-and-a-half she couldn't remember anything about it, although she spoke Hebrew well. She stayed at Uncle Àrmin and Aunt Sosanna's house for two weeks. Their door was always open for relatives. After that she found a kibbutz not far from Tel Aviv and fell in love with the kibbutz life. She ended up staying in Israel for six months instead of two, and our phone bill was higher for those six months than her return ticket to Israel. Finally, she came home after a truly wonderful trip. We had worried a lot when she was in Israel and were relieved to have her home.

Epilogue

I began writing this book in the year 2000 and it took approximately two years of concentrated effort to write my life story from my birth in Hungary to our early years in Canada. Much of this writing was difficult and tiring, so I decided to end my memoir with the year 1978. At that time I was forty-seven years old and we had been in Canada for eight years.

Since 1978, many things have happened in my family. My lovely Judit and I have had so many experiences – in business, our social life, travel and in life itself. We returned many times to the Holy Land of Israel, but the journey that we took in the winter of 1979 was the one that I remember the most because of the spectacular things we saw at the foot of Mount Moses (Gebel Musa), now most commonly known as Mount Sinai. The large valley at the foot of the mountain easily accommodated the Israelites of the time when Moses received the Ten Commandments from God.

On February 29, 1979, we took a flight to the Sinai Desert in a small two-engine airplane with a group of about forty people, landing on a small airstrip about a one-hour bus ride from the monastery of Santa Katarina, or Saint Catherine. The monastery, which sits at the bottom of Mount Sinai, is splendid – it is quite big and has a history that goes back more than 1,400 years, to the earliest part of the Christian era.

Many monks and hermits settled in the nearby Oasis of Feiran (Wadi Feiran) in those early years of Christianity, building tiny cells in the gullies and on the cliffs. It was in Feiran that Israel faced its first hostile attack under Moses and the same nomadic tribes gave the monks of Sinai no peace; many of them lost their lives in these repeated incursions. In a big room in the basement of Saint Catherine's monastery, we saw hundreds of skulls in organized piles – the skulls of the numerous monks who had died there so long ago.

The monastery church has stained glass windows showing Old Testament images such as Moses with the Ten Commandments. I felt almost as if I were in an old synagogue, where Abraham went to sacrifice his son Isaac and instead found a lamb to place on the altar.

Saint Catherine's monastery was constructed around a small fourth-century chapel that was built about forty kilometres south of the Oasis of Feiran, on the spot at the foot of Mount Sinai believed to be where, according to the Bible, Moses encountered the burning bush: "And he looked and behold the bush burned with fire and the bush was not consumed" (Exodus 3:4). When our bus left Saint Catherine's, looking out the bus window on a hilltop not far from the monastery, Judit and I actually saw with our own eyes a burning bush – it was very real, appeared to be on fire and still was not consumed! That bush, although not the biblically associated bush growing on the site of Saint Catherine's monastery (*Rubus sanctus*), was most likely the *Loranthus acaciae*: the "flames" come from the crimson blossoms of the mistletoe twigs. My not-very-scientific explanation is that when you look at the bush, thinking of God and his holiness, and the sun lights it up in a mass of brilliant flaming colour, the bush appears to be on fire. It appears to burn and not be consumed.

Our tour of Saint Catherine's monastery lasted a good half a day and as we drove away in the bus we saw a group of about fifty people wearing *tallitot*, or prayer shawls. The people all seemed to be praying. As we got closer, I saw that they were Japanese and the tour guide told us that they were Jewish converts who had come to pray at the foot of

Mount Moses. There are approximately five to six hundred Japanese Jews who were converted by one Japanese believer after World War II. We couldn't stop to talk to them because they were deep in prayer, praying on the very spot where, it is believed, the Israelites waited for Moses to come down from the mountain with the two stone tablets containing the Ten Commandments. That was an unforgettable encounter with yet another kind of Jews.

We travelled back to the airstrip through the Sinai Desert and the view of that vast wasteland brought back memories of what had happened there twenty-three years ago when I was a soldier in the 1956 Sinai War. Instead of being a tourist on a bus, I was sitting in a tank on what was probably the same road. The landscape had not changed at all. Our trip ended when we flew back to Tel Aviv from the old Jerusalem airport.

Judit, her cousin Vera, Vera's husband, Peter Foltin, and I went on another interesting trip to the archaeological site near Megiddo, Israel. Peter is a wonderful warm-hearted man, full of love for his whole family, who passed away at the young age of fifty-six. I had the good fortune to get to know him when we stayed with them in Haifa on the gorgeous Mount Carmel. Peter was our official tour guide of the mountains, taking us from Haifa through many prosperous Arab and Druze villages. All the villages had excellent restaurants with healthy, organic Middle Eastern foods that were popular with many Israelis.

After two hours of driving we arrived at Megiddo (Tell el-Mutesellim), which was a small fortified town in the time of the Canaanites. The whole town sat on only about five hectares of land, on a hill overlooking the fertile Jezreel Valley (Emek Jezreel). The valley extends from the mountains of Galilee in the north to Samaria and is mentioned many times in the Bible. Located on one of the ancient trade routes, Megiddo played a very important role in trade and commerce because it had access to a good water supply from a stream deep in the earth. We were able to go about twelve metres underground, where we saw for ourselves the wonderful stream of clean fresh water.

We also visited the town of Taanach, just over eight kilometres from Megiddo, that is mentioned in the biblical victory hymn, "The Song of Deborah." Numerous battles took place on the broad plain of Jezreel and two mounds of rubble are all that is left of both Taanach and Megiddo.

The next day we travelled to see Beit She'an, strategically located at the junction of the Jordan River Valley and the Jezreel Valley, where King Saul lost the battle against the Philistines. The great mound of rubble there – Tell Beit-She'an or Tel el-Hosn (mound of the fortress) – is visible far beyond the Jordan Valley.

During the many hours that the four of us wandered amid the ruins of Beit She'an, we saw an interesting excavation in which a Greek bathing house and an amphitheatre were just beginning to show their shapes. The sun was very strong, but we drank plenty of water and we rested a few minutes every hour of walking. That evening we went back through the city of Afula and ate a wonderful dinner in Haifa, in Vera and Peter's Carmel home. This was another trip to remember forever.

The most rewarding and moving events in the years after I ended this memoir were the marriages of our beautiful Iris to a wonderful young man, Darrel Yashinsky, in 1983, and our beloved son, Paul, to Gitta Katz in 1988, and the births of our six loving grandchildren Jordan, Noah, Joshua, Dalia Leona, Elan and Daniel.

And there have been so many changes in the world and in Israel.

Many years have passed since the Holocaust and the time I spent in hiding as a teenager, but I know I'll never forget what happened during those years. My only regret is that I was not able to see the dangers coming in the time leading up to the war. My fellow Jews had told me over and over again that Hungarian Jews were safe and would be safe in the future, too. They continued preaching that same message, even as the Polish Jews were taken to the death camps.

I feel now that had I been older I would have done something to open the eyes of my fellow Jews and my whole family. Now, in my later years, I often feel helplessness and regret that I was too young at the time to fight the Nazis and had no knowledge of an underground resistance group in Hungary.

I have often contemplated what would have been different in my life if the Holocaust hadn't happened, if I had had a different education or perhaps a different occupation. Perhaps I could have had a PhD or even an MD. In my youth I loved politics and debating, so I guess if things had been different, if we hadn't been forced to leave our homes, I could've done almost anything.

Today, I feel if God will give me enough health and strength, I will write another book to express my opinions about all these matters.

LEHITRAOT BEKAROV!

SEE YOU SOON!

Glossary

aliyah (Hebrew; pl. *aliyot*, literally, ascent) A term used by Jews and modern Israelis to refer to Jewish immigration to Israel; the term is also used to refer to "going up" to the altar in a synagogue to read from the Torah.

antisemitism Prejudice, discrimination, persecution and/or hatred against Jewish people, institutions, culture and symbols.

Arrow Cross Party (Hungarian; *Nyilaskeresztes Párt – Hungarista Mozgalom*; abbreviation: Nyilas) A Hungarian nationalistic and antisemitic party founded by Ferenc Szálasi in 1935 under the name the Party of National Will. With the full support of Nazi Germany, the newly renamed Arrow Cross Party ran in Hungary's 1939 election and won 25 per cent of the vote. The party was banned shortly after the elections, but was legalized again in March 1944 when Germany occupied Hungary. Under Nazi approval, the party assumed control of Hungary from October 15, 1944, to March 1945, led by Szálasi under the name the Government of National Unity. The Arrow Cross regime was particularly brutal toward Jews – in addition to the thousands of Hungarian Jews who had been deported to Nazi death camps during the previous Miklós Horthy regime, the Arrow Cross, during their short period of rule, instigated the murder of tens of thousands of Hungarian Jews. In one specific incident on November 8, 1944, more than 70,000 Jews were rounded up and sent on a death march to

Nazi camps in Austria. Between December 1944 and January 1945, the Arrow Cross murdered approximately 20,000 Jews, many of whom had been forced into a closed ghetto at the end of November 1944. *See also* Budapest ghetto; Horthy, Miklós.

Ashkenazi (Hebrew) An adjective first used in the Middle Ages to describe Jews of Germanic descent; in the eleventh century, the term also came to encompass Jews of Central and Eastern European descent. *See also* Sephardic.

Auschwitz (German; in Polish, Oświęcim) A town in southern Poland approximately forty kilometres from Krakow, it is also the name of the largest complex of Nazi concentration camps that were built nearby. The Auschwitz complex contained three main camps: Auschwitz I, a slave labour camp built in May 1940; Auschwitz II-Birkenau, a death camp built in early 1942; and Auschwitz-Monowitz, a slave labour camp built in October 1942. In 1941, Auschwitz I was a testing site for usage of the lethal gas Zyklon B as a method of mass killing, which then went into wide usage. Between May 15 and July 8, 1944, approximately 435,000 Hungarian Jews were deported to Auschwitz, where an estimated 1.1 million people were murdered. Approximately 950,000 of the people killed were Jewish; 74,000 Polish; 21,000 Roma; 15,000 Soviet prisoners of war; and 10,000–15,000 other nationalities. The Auschwitz complex was liberated by the Soviet army in January 1945.

bar mitzvah (Hebrew; literally, one to whom commandments apply) The age of thirteen when, according to Jewish tradition, boys become religiously and morally responsible for their actions and are considered adults for the purpose of synagogue ritual. A bar mitzvah is also the synagogue ceremony and family celebration that mark the attainment of this status, during which the boy is called upon to read a portion of the Torah and recite the prescribed prayers in a public prayer forum. In the latter half of the twentieth century, liberal Jews instituted an equivalent ceremony and celebration for girls called a bat mitzvah.

Bergen-Belsen A concentration camp initially established by the Nazis in 1940 for prisoners of war near Celle, Germany. After 1943, it held so-called exchange Jews, whom Germany hoped to use in peace negotiations with the Allies. After March 1944, part of the camp was designated as a "recovery camp" and one thousand prisoners from Mittelbau-Dora and other forced labour camps who were too sick to work were sent to Bergen-Belsen. They did not receive any treatment, and instead were left to die from starvation and disease. Toward the end of the war, thousands of prisoners from camps close to the front lines, such as Auschwitz, Mittelbau-Dora and Buchenwald were taken there, as were forced labourers from Hungary. With the influx of inmates, camp conditions deteriorated rapidly and some 35,000 people died there between January and April 1945. British forces liberated the camp on April 15, 1945.

Betar A Zionist youth movement founded by Revisionist Zionist leader Ze'ev Jabotinsky in 1923 that encouraged the development of a new generation of Zionist activists based on the ideals of courage, self-respect, military training, defence of Jewish life and property, and settlement in Israel to establish a Jewish state in British Mandate Palestine. During the 1930s and 1940s, as antisemitism increased and the Nazis launched their murderous campaign against the Jews of Europe, Betar rescued thousands of Jews by organizing illegal immigration to British Mandate Palestine. The Betar movement today, closely aligned with Israel's right-wing Likud party, remains involved in supporting Jewish and Zionist activism around the world. *See also* Jabotinsky, Ze'ev.

Bricha (Hebrew; literally, escape) The name given to the massive, organized, clandestine migration of Jews from Eastern Europe and DP camps to pre-state Israel following World War II. Estimates of the number of Jews helped by Bricha range from 80,000 to 250,000.

brit milah (Hebrew; in Yiddish, bris; literally, covenant of circumcision) Judaism's religious ceremony to welcome male infants into the covenant between God and the Children of Israel through a ritual circumcision (removal of the foreskin of the penis) performed by a mohel, or circumciser, eight days after the baby is born. Traditionally, a baby boy is named after his brit milah. *See also* circumcision.

British Broadcasting Corporation (BBC) The British public service broadcaster. During World War II, the BBC broadcast radio programming to Europe in German and the languages of the occupied countries. Allied forces used some of this programming to send coded messages to resistance groups. It was illegal to listen to these broadcasts, but many people in Nazi-occupied Europe turned to it as the most reliable source of news.

British Mandate Palestine The area of the Middle East under British rule from 1923 to 1948, as established by the League of Nations after World War I. During that time, the United Kingdom severely restricted Jewish immigration. The Mandate area encompassed present-day Israel, Jordan, the West Bank and the Gaza Strip.

Buda The western part of Budapest, situated west of the Danube River. The area comprises about one-third of Budapest and is mostly hilly and wooded. *See also* Pest and the map on page xxvii.

Budapest ghetto The ghetto established by the government of Hungary on November 29, 1944. By December 10, the ghetto and its 33,000 Jewish inhabitants were sealed off from the rest of the city. At the end of December, Jews who had previously held "protected" status (many by the Swedish government) were moved into the ghetto, and the number of residents increased to 55,000; by January 1945, the number had reached 70,000. The ghetto was overcrowded and lacked sufficient food, water and sanitation. Supplies dwindled and conditions worsened during the Soviet siege of Budapest and thousands died of starvation and disease. Soviet forces liberated the ghetto on January 18, 1945. *See also* ghetto; Swedish legation (Budapest).

Chanukah (also Hanukah; Hebrew; dedication) An eight-day festival celebrated in December to mark the victory of the Jews against foreign conquerors who desecrated the Temple in Jerusalem in the second century B C E. Traditionally, each night of Chanukah is marked by lighting an eight-branch candelabrum called a menorah to commemorate the rededication of the Temple and the miracle of its lamp burning for eight days without oil.

Chasam Sofer (1762–1839) Also known as Rabbi Moshe Sofer, the Chasam Sofer was the Orthodox leader of the Jewish community of Pressburg (Bratislava) from 1806 until his death. His book on Jewish law, *Chasam Sofer* (Seal of the Scribe), which was published posthumously and gives his title, is still widely referenced today.

chassene (Yiddish) Wedding.

cheder (Hebrew; literally, room) An Orthodox Jewish elementary school that teaches the fundamentals of Jewish religious observance and textual study, as well as the Hebrew language.

cholent (Yiddish) A traditional Jewish slow-cooked pot stew usually eaten as the main course at the festive Shabbat lunch on Saturdays after the synagogue service and on other Jewish holidays. For Jews of Eastern-European descent, the basic ingredients of *cholent* are meat, potatoes, beans and barley.

chuppah (Hebrew; literally, covering) The canopy used in traditional Jewish weddings that is usually made of a cloth (sometimes a prayer shawl) stretched or supported over four poles. It is meant to symbolize the home the couple will build together.

circumcision Removal of the foreskin of the penis. In Judaism, ritual circumcision is performed on the eighth day of a male infant's life in a religious ceremony known as a *brit milah* (Hebrew) or *bris* (Yiddish) to welcome him into the covenant between God and the People of Israel. *See also* brit milah.

cohen (Hebrew; pl. *cohanim*) In biblical times, the word for priest. The *cohanim* were responsible for worship ceremonies in the days of the Temple in Jerusalem. In the post-biblical era, a *cohen* refers to a male Jew who can trace his ancestry to the family of Judaism's first priest, Aaron, the brother of Moses. *Cohanim* occupy a special ritual status in Judaism (such as reciting certain blessings in synagogues). According to Jewish tradition, particular rules apply to a *cohen*, such as having no contact with dead bodies and not marrying a divorcee or a convert to Judaism.

Cyprus An island nation in the Mediterranean and former British colony that was granted independence from Great Britain in 1960. In the 1940s, Cyprus was the location of British detention camps for European Jewish refugees who were attempting to illegally immigrate to British Mandate Palestine. More than 50,000 Jewish refugees were interned in these camps. *See also* British Mandate Palestine.

Faluja pocket The term for the area comprising the Arab villages of Al-Faluja and Iraq al-Manshiyya that was the site of a number of battles and a four-month long siege of Egyptian troops by Israeli forces during the War of Independence, also known as the 1948 Arab-Israeli War. Under the February 1949 armistice agreement, the area was transferred to Israel. *See also* War of Independence.

ghetto A confined residential area for Jews. The term originated in Venice, Italy in 1516 with a law requiring all Jews to live on a segregated, gated island known as Ghetto Nuovo. Throughout the Middle Ages in Europe, Jews were often forcibly confined to gated Jewish neighbourhoods. During the Holocaust, the Nazis forced Jews to live in crowded and unsanitary conditions in rundown districts of cities and towns.

gimnázium (Hungarian; in German, *Gymnasium*) A word used throughout Central and Eastern Europe to mean high school or secondary school.

Haggadah (Hebrew; literally, telling) A book of readings that lays out the order of the Passover seder and recounts the biblical exodus from slavery. *See also* Passover; seder.

Horthy, Miklós (1868–1957) The regent of Hungary during the interwar period and for much of World War II. Horthy presided over a government that was aligned with the Axis powers and supported Nazi ideology. After the German army occupied Hungary in March 1944, Horthy served primarily as a figurehead to the pro-Nazi government; nevertheless, he was able to order the suspension of the deportation of Hungarian Jews to death camps in the beginning of July 1944. Horthy planned to withdraw his country from the war on October 15, 1944, but the Nazis supported an Arrow Cross coup that same day and forced Horthy to abdicate. *See also* Arrow Cross Party.

Hungarian Revolution (1956) A spontaneous uprising against the Soviet-backed Communist government of Hungary in October 1956, the Hungarian Revolution led to the brief establishment of a reformist government under Prime Minister Imre Nagy. The revolution was swiftly crushed by the Soviet invasion of November 1956, during which thousands of civilians were killed.

Jabotinsky, Ze'ev (1880–1940) The founder of the Revisionist Zionist movement. In 1935, Jabotinsky established his own branch of nationalist Zionism, the New Zionist Organization, which advocated Jewish self-defence and self-determination. Jabotinsky strongly urged European Jews to immigrate to British Mandate Palestine and met with the governments of Hungary, Poland and Romania to lobby this "evacuation plan." He believed in establishing a Jewish state in Palestine with the support of Jewish brigades. Jabotinsky was also commander of the Irgun, the underground Jewish military organization that operated in Palestine between 1937 and 1948. *See also* Betar.

Kálmán, Emmerich (Imre) (1882–1953) Hungarian-Jewish composer of operettas.

kocsonya hal (Hungarian; fish jelly) A traditional, gelatinous Hungarian meal usually made from pork.

kosher (Hebrew) Fit to eat according to Jewish dietary laws. Observant Jews follow a system of rules known as *kashruth* that regulates what can be eaten, how food is prepared and how meat and poultry are slaughtered. Food is kosher when it has been deemed fit for consumption according to this system of rules. There are several foods that are forbidden, most notably pork products and shellfish.

Maariv (Hebrew) The evening Jewish prayer service. *See also* Mincha; Shacharit.

Magen David (Hebrew; in English, Star of David) The six-pointed star that is the ancient and most recognizable symbol of Judaism. During World War II, many Jews in Nazi-occupied areas were forced to wear a badge or armband with the Star of David on it as an identifying mark of their lesser status and to single them out as targets for persecution.

matzah (Hebrew; also matza, matzoh, matsah; in Yiddish, matze) Crisp flatbread made of plain white flour and water that is not allowed to rise before or during baking. Matzah is the substitute for bread during the Jewish holiday of Passover, when eating bread and leavened products is forbidden. *See also* Passover.

miluim (Hebrew) The Israeli army annual reserve duty that lasts between twenty and thirty days. Israelis currently serve in the Israel Defense Forces from age eighteen to twenty (for women) or twenty-one (for men). Following their mandatory service, Israelis are required to attend *miluim* until the age of forty or fifty, depending on their prior position in the military.

Mincha (Hebrew) The afternoon Jewish prayer service. *See also* Maariv; Shacharit.

minyan (Hebrew) The quorum of ten adult male Jews required for certain religious rites. The term can also designate a congregation.

mitzvah (Hebrew; commanded deed) A fundamental Jewish concept about the obligation of Jews to perform the commandments set forth in the Torah; mainly used to mean "good deed" or "act of kindness."

Mizrachi (acronym of Merkaz Ruchani; Hebrew, spiritual centre) An

Orthodox nationalist Zionist movement founded in Vilna, Lithuania in 1902. Mizrachi was founded on the belief that the Torah is central to Zionism and Jewish life. The movement's principles are encompassed in its slogan "The land of Israel for the people of Israel according to the Torah of Israel." *See also* Zionism.

moshav (Hebrew; literally, settlement or village) An agricultural cooperative comprised of individually-owned farms that was founded by the Labour Zionist movement in the early twentieth century.

Nasser, Abdel Gamal (1918–1970) Deputy commander of Egypt's troops in the area known as the Faluja pocket during the 1948 War of Independence, Nasser served as president of Egypt from 1956 until his death in 1970. *See also* Faluja pocket; War of Independence.

Neolog Judaism A reform movement that emerged from the 1868 Hungarian Jewish Congress. Neolog Jews were more liberal and secular than Orthodox Jews and spoke Hungarian rather than Yiddish as their first language. In present-day Hungary, most of the remaining, small Jewish community belong to Neolog synagogues. *See also* Orthodox Judaism; Yiddish.

Nyilas. *See* Arrow Cross Party.

Orthodox Judaism The set of beliefs and practices of Jews for whom the observance of Jewish law is closely connected to faith; it is characterized by strict religious observance of Jewish dietary laws, restrictions on work on the Sabbath and holidays, and a modest code of dress.

Passover (in Hebrew, Pesach) One of the major festivals of the Jewish calendar. Passover commemorates the liberation and exodus of the Israelite slaves from Egypt during the reign of the Pharaoh Ramses II. Occurring in the spring, the festival lasts for eight days and begins with a lavish ritual meal called a seder during which the story of Exodus is retold through the reading of a Jewish religious text called the Haggadah. With its special foods, songs and customs, the seder is the focal point of the Passover celebration and is traditionally a time of family gathering. During Passover, Jews refrain from eating *chametz* – that is, anything that contains barley, wheat, rye, oats, and spelt that has undergone fermentation as a result of contact with liquid. The name of the festival refers to the fact that God "passed over" the houses of the Jews when He set about slaying the firstborn sons of Egypt as the last of the ten plagues aimed at convincing Pharaoh to free the Jews. *See also* Haggadah; matzah; seder.

Pest The mostly flat, commercial, eastern part of Budapest divided from Buda by the Danube River. It comprises about two-thirds of the city. *See also* Buda.

Purim (Hebrew; literally, lots) The celebration of the Jews' escape from annihilation in Persia. The Purim story recounts how Haman, advisor to the King of Persia, planned to rid Persia of Jews, and how Queen Esther and her cousin Mordecai foiled Haman's plot by convincing the king to save the Jews. During the Purim festivities, people dress up as one of the figures in the Purim story, hold parades and retell the story of Haman, Esther and Mordecai.

Rabbinical Seminary of Budapest A teaching institution established in 1877 that followed the Neolog strain of Judaism, combining general education courses with classical rabbinical studies. In 1944, during the Nazi occupation of Hungary, the seminary was closed and converted into a prison, from where Jews were deported to Nazi camps. After the war, the seminary became a graduate institution for both rabbis and Hebrew teachers. It existed throughout the Communist era and still exists today, as the Budapest University of Jewish Studies.

Rosh Hashanah (Hebrew; New Year) The autumn holiday that marks the beginning of the Jewish year and ushers in the High Holy Days. It is observed by a synagogue service that ends with blowing the *shofar* (ram's horn), marking the beginning of the holiday. The service is usually followed by a family dinner where sweet foods, such as apples and honey, are eaten to symbolize and celebrate a sweet new year.

seder (Hebrew; literally, order) A ritual family meal celebrated at the beginning of the festival of Passover. *See also* Passover.

Sephardic (Hebrew) The adjective used to describe Sephardim, Jews of Spanish, Portuguese or North African descent. The word derives from the biblical name for a country that is taken to be Spain.

Shabbat (Hebrew; in Yiddish, Shabbes, Shabbos; in English, Sabbath) The weekly day of rest beginning Friday at sunset and ending Saturday at sundown ushered in by the lighting of candles on Friday night and the recitation of blessings over wine and challah (egg bread); a day of celebration as well as prayer, it is customary to eat three festive meals, attend synagogue services and refrain from doing any work or travelling.

Shacharit The morning Jewish prayer service. *See also* Maariv; Mincha.

Shema Yisrael (Hebrew; "Hear, O Israel") The first two words of a section of the Torah and an extremely important prayer in Judaism. The full verse, "Hear, O Israel: the Lord is our God, the Lord is one," refers to faith and loyalty in one God, which is the essence of Judaism. The Shema prayer comprises three verses in the Torah and observant Jews recite the Shema twice daily, morning and evening.

shtiebl (Yiddish; little house or little room) A small, unadorned prayer room or prayer house furnished more modestly than a synagogue. Most observant Jews in Eastern Europe prayed in *shtiebls* on a daily basis; they attended services in a synagogue on holidays or sometimes on Shabbat. *See also* Shabbat.

simcha (Hebrew; gladness, joy) Generally refers to a festive occasion.

Six-Day War The armed conflict between Israel and the neighbouring states of Egypt, Jordan and Syria that took place from June 5–10, 1967. In response to Egypt closing the Straits of Tiran to Israeli shipping, the creation of an alliance between Egypt, Syria

and Jordan, and the mobilization of troops by Egypt's leader Gamal Nasser along Israel's borders, Israel launched a pre-emptive
attack. In the days that followed, Israeli forces drove the armies
back and occupied the Sinai Peninsula, Gaza Strip, West Bank and
Golan Heights. Israel also reunited Jerusalem, the eastern half of
which Jordan had controlled since the 1948–1949 war.

Sochnut (Hebrew; abbreviation of HaSochnut HaYehudit L'Eretz
Yisrael; in English, Jewish Agency for Israel) The organization
established by the World Zionist Organization in 1929 that was
largely responsible for economic and cultural development of pre-
state Israel, as well as immigration and supporting resettlement of
immigrants. The Sochnut's main current function is facilitating
immigration to Israel.

Suez Crisis Also known as the Tripartite Aggression, Sinai War and
the Second Arab-Israeli War. The October and November 1956
conflict between Egypt and Israel, France and Britain over the
ownership of the Suez Canal, an essential route for oil shipments.
Mediated by the first-ever United Nations Emergency Force, the
conflict ended with Israel's withdrawal of troops in March 1957.

Swedish legation (Budapest) The office where Swedish diplomat
Raoul Wallenberg (1912–1947?) worked between July and December 1944. The Swedish government authorized Wallenberg to issue protective passes to tens of thousands of Budapest Jews and
set up "safe houses," buildings designated as Swedish territory and
thus protected by the Swedish government. Of the slightly more
than 100,000 Jews who remained alive in Budapest at the end of
the war (out of a pre-war population of 247,000), the majority
were saved through Wallenberg's efforts. Wallenberg was awarded
the title of Righteous Among the Nations by Yad Vashem in 1986
and has been honoured by memorials or monuments in ten other
countries.

Talmud (Hebrew; literally, instruction or learning) An ancient rabbinic text that discusses Jewish history, law and ethics, the Talmud is comprised of two sections: the Mishnah, which is further subdivided into six sections and focuses on legal issues, and the Gemara, which analyzes the legal issues. *See also* Torah.

Tarbut (Hebrew; literally, culture) A Zionist network of secular Hebrew-language schools – kindergartens, elementary schools, secondary schools and adult education programs – that operated primarily in Poland, Romania and Lithuania between World War I and World War II. The name Tarbut references the schools' secular and cultural approach to Jewish studies as opposed to religious instruction. The educational institutions under the Tarbut umbrella also included teachers' seminaries, lending libraries and a publishing house that produced pedagogical materials, textbooks and children's periodicals.

tefillin (Hebrew) Phylacteries. A pair of black leather boxes containing scrolls of parchment inscribed with Bible verses and worn by Jews on the arm and forehead at prescribed times of prayer as a symbol of the covenantal relationship with God.

Theresienstadt (German; in Czech, Terezin) A walled town in the Czech Republic sixty kilometres north of Prague that served as both a ghetto and a concentration camp. More than 73,000 Jews from the German Protectorate of Bohemia and Moravia and from the Greater German Reich (including Austria and parts of Poland) were deported to Terezin between 1941 and 1945, 60,000 of whom were deported to Auschwitz or other death camps. Terezin was showcased as a "model" ghetto for propaganda purposes to demonstrate to delegates from the International Red Cross and others the "humane" treatment of Jews and to counter information reaching the Allies about Nazi atrocities and mass murder. Theresienstadt was liberated on May 8, 1945 by the Soviet army.

Torah (Hebrew) The Five Books of Moses (the first five books of the Bible), also called the Pentateuch. The Torah is the core of Jewish scripture, traditionally believed to have been given to Moses on Mount Sinai. In Christianity it is referred to as the "Old Testament." *See also* Talmud.

Tzena (Hebrew; austerity) The measures adopted by the Israeli government between 1949 and 1959 to ration food and other supplies to Israel's burgeoning immigrant population that had doubled since the creation of the State of Israel in May 1948. Citizens used ration coupons for a variety of goods until 1953, when most austerity measures were cancelled due to the post-war reparations agreement with Germany that boosted the economy. Some of the restrictions continued until 1959.

ulpan (Hebrew; pl. *ulpanim*) A school that offers an intensive Hebrew-language study program. *Ulpanim*, the first of which was established in Jerusalem in 1949, were created to help new immigrants learn the language of their new country and acclimatize to its culture.

War of Independence Also known as the 1948 Arab-Israeli War or the first Arab-Israeli War. The conflict between the state of Israel and Arab forces after Israel's independence was declared on May 14, 1948.

Vietnam War The conflict between North Vietnam and US-supported South Vietnam that took place between November 1955 and April 1975.

Yemenite Jews Jews originally from the country of Yemen. Between 1949 and 1950, approximately 50,000 Jews immigrated to Israel from Yemen, where they were suffering from persecution and pogroms.

yeshiva (Hebrew) A Jewish educational institution in which religious texts such as the Torah and Talmud are studied. *See also* Talmud; Torah.

Yiddish A language derived from Middle High German with elements of Hebrew, Aramaic, Romance and Slavic languages, and written in Hebrew characters. Spoken by Jews in east-central Europe for roughly a thousand years from the tenth century to the mid-twentieth century, it was still the most common language among European Jews until the outbreak of World War II. There are similarities between Yiddish and contemporary German.

Zionism A movement promoted by the Viennese Jewish journalist Theodor Herzl, who argued in his 1896 book *Der Judenstaat* (The Jewish State) that the best way to resolve the problem of anti-semitism and persecution of Jews in Europe was to create an independent Jewish state in the historic Jewish homeland of Biblical Israel. Zionists also promoted the revival of Hebrew as a Jewish national language.

Photographs

1 George Stern's paternal grandparents, Bertha (née Fleischman) and Fülöp Stern.
2 George Stern's mother, Leona Stern (right), with her sisters Rózsi (centre) and Jolán (left).

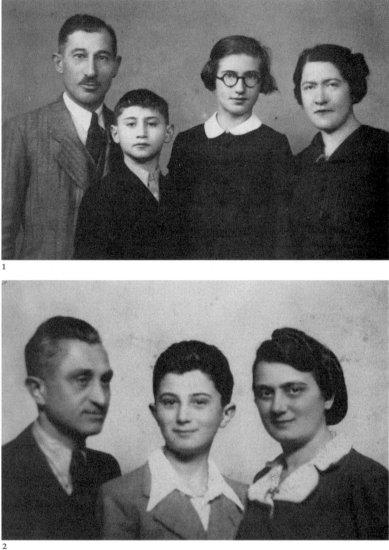

1 George Stern (second from the left) with his father, Ernő (left), his sister, Ágnes (second from the right) and his mother, Leona (right).

2 George Stern's paternal uncle Jenő, cousin Iván and aunt Lili.

A page from the Swedish passport that allowed George Stern and his father, Ernő, to seek refuge in one of the "safe" houses under the protection of the Swedish legation in Budapest in the fall of 1944.

Judit (Katz) Stern's family in the "yellow-star house" in the Budapest ghetto in 1944. From left to right: Judit's sister Klara; her mother, Blanka; her sister Éva; her father, Izidor (Israel); and Judit.

1 George Stern, age nineteen, in the Israeli army.
2 George Stern (third from the right) with friends in the Israeli army, 1949.

George Stern and Judit Katz's wedding photo. Ramat Gan, Israel, August 16, 1951.

1 George Stern's sister, Ágnes, with her husband, Endre Szàntó, and their two children, Tomàs and Annetta.

2 George Stern aboard the ship to Brazil, September 1960.

1 George and Judit Stern at the reception for Zalman Shazar, president of Israel,
   with the wife of the ambassador to Togo. São Paulo, Brazil, 1966.
2 George, Judit, Iris and Paul Stern in their new apartment in São Paulo, 1968.

1   Iris, Judit and Paul Stern in Los Angeles, 1970.

2   The Stern family in Toronto, 1975. From left to right (behind): Paul, George and Iris Stern; in front (seated): Judit Stern.

1 Iris Stern and Darrel Yashinsky's wedding, Toronto, 1983. From left to right: George Stern, Judit Stern, Iris Stern and Darrel Yashinsky.
2 George Stern's paternal uncle Àrmin Stern and his wife, Sosanna, at Iris Stern's wedding, Toronto, 1983.

1 The memorial stone for George Stern's mother, Leona Stern, (middle row, second from the top) in the Lipa Green Centre in Toronto.

2 George Stern holding a memorial banner honouring his parents, Leona and Arnold Stern, and Judit Stern's parents, Israel and Blanka Katz. Beth Tikvah, Toronto, c. 2004.

George Stern with Israeli ambassador Alan Baker at Mizrachi Canada's 1948 War Veterans' Tribute during celebrations for the 60th anniversary of the founding of the State of Israel. Toronto, 2008.

Index

The Azrieli Foundation was established in 1989 to realize and extend the philanthropic vision of David J. Azrieli, C.M., C.Q., M.Arch. The Foundation's mission is to support a wide spectrum of initiatives in education and research. The Azrieli Foundation is an active supporter of programs in the fields of Jewish education, the education of architects, scientific and medical research, and education in the arts. The Azrieli Foundation's many well-known initiatives include: the Holocaust Survivor Memoirs Program, which collects, preserves, publishes and distributes the written memoirs of survivors in Canada; the Azrieli Institute for Educational Empowerment, an innovative program successfully working to keep at-risk youth in school; and the Azrieli Fellows Program, which promotes academic excellence and leadership on the graduate level at Israeli universities.